LONELY PLANET'S

INSTANT EXPERT

A Visual Guide to the Skills You've Always Wanted

NIGEL HOLMES

To Erin, my love, my friend

LONELY PLANET'S
INSTANT
EXPERT

A Visual Guide to the Skills You've Always Wanted

NIGEL HOLMES

NIGEL HOLMES

CONTENTS

CONTENTS

Introduction

This book is named after **twin bees:**
Instant Bee and **Expert Bee.**

Instant Bee skims the surface of a subject, flitting from one to another, taking just enough to satisfy itself.

Instant Bee takes the stuff back to the hive where Expert Bee turns it (we hope) into a delicious spread.

(And who knows, you might learn something here that will be useful when travelling. It might even lead you to an interesting and adventurous new life!)

Maori cook   Parasitologist   Weather guru   Casanova   Mountain guide   Origamist

Both bees are important to the project, even though you might think that Instant Bee is a shallow dilettante, especially compared to hard-working Expert Bee. (In truth, Instant Bee thinks that Expert Bee is a bit of a pedant.)

Indeed, the twin bees realize that they need each other: the value of what they do is what they do **together**. And together they produce just the thing for a lively dinner party conversation. It's not really "How to be an origamist, or a caber tosser" but rather "How to chat about being an origamist" (or a caber tosser). You know, fun, without going on too long about it.

Caber tosser? What's that?

Just read the book!

Now the bees do know the difference between real-life experts and instant experts. Almost all the jobs, professions and careers here usually take tons of time, energy, training and experience to get to "expert" status.

I mean, how could a book like this pretend to make you, dear reader, an expert in sailing, or emergency dentistry, or beekeeping, in the space of a few pages?

Perhaps a few of you will become Jacks or Jills of all trades (even if you are masters of none). Thank goodness for "instant"—it takes a lot of the burden away from "expert".

Like inseparable twins—always together, nothing without each other—the bees ask the old question: are there two bees, or not two bees?

With apologies to William Shakesbee.

PRACTICAL TRAVELLER

Bouncer

Ahem, **Crowd-controller** or **Security Guard** is the preferred term, sir.
Bouncers have had a bad rep but the job is more professional now
and depends more on "dispute resolution" than being a bully. Wearing a dark
suit and tie
suggests authority—
you aren't one of
the guys trying
to get in.

Basically
it's **two** jobs:

1 Keeping order OUTSIDE (deciding who gets in)

- Control the entrance using the red rope. **This is your domain.** The red rope keeps the queue from becoming a crush.

- **Treat everyone as you would like to be treated.** Be polite and flattering at the start of a night and it'll pay off if you have to diffuse tensions later.

- To refuse entry, cite the **dress code** or say it's a **private party.**

- **Don't accept tips or handshakes.**

- Be wary of overly friendly people.

- Watch out for deliberate distractions.

- **Check IDs.** If you think someone is underage or using a fake ID, ask them their birthdate and zodiac sign.

- **Don't let insults aggravate you**—practise by getting a friend to insult you. Be aware of your body language.

2 Keeping order INSIDE
(deciding who gets thrown out)

- **Expect the unexpected.**

- Looking out for drunken people is a big part of the job.

- **Take it outside.**

- The essence of being a good bouncer is to **handle difficult situations without resorting to violence.**

- So ... be nice until it's time to be not nice.

- Point out surveillance cameras, and win over the drunken person's friends.

- **Talk first** before throwing anyone out. Redirect their attention. If there are other bouncers working, get them to help and **approach troublemakers in a triangle formation.**

- **Never show fear.** Look your aggressor in the eyes.

- Have the **police on speed dial.**

Launderer

Ever wondered what the tiny symbols on those annoying tags on your clothes really mean? As a launderer, you'd better find out! (and, if you are doing laundry for someone else, just pray they haven't snipped the tags off.)

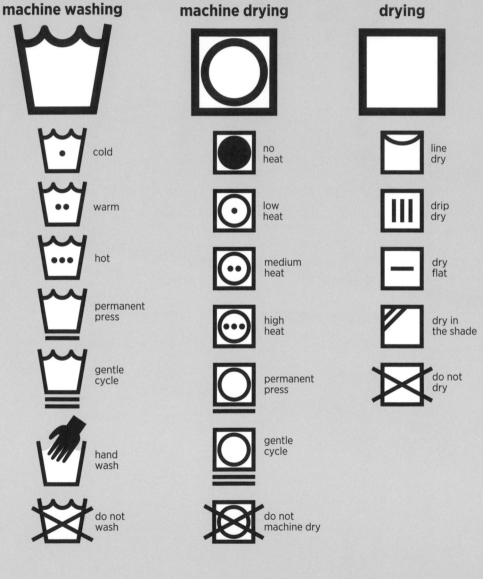

machine washing

- cold
- warm
- hot
- permanent press
- gentle cycle
- hand wash
- do not wash

machine drying

- no heat
- low heat
- medium heat
- high heat
- permanent press
- gentle cycle
- do not machine dry

drying

- line dry
- drip dry
- dry flat
- dry in the shade
- do not dry

bleaching

any
bleach

only
non-chlorine
bleach

do not
bleach

ironing

steam
or dry,
low
heat

steam
or dry,
medium
heat

steam
or dry,
high
heat

do not
iron wih
steam

do not
iron

dry cleaning

any
solvent

any
solvent
except
trichloro-
ethylene

do not
dry clean

and ...

- a little **nail polish remover** gets rid of lipstick stains
- **white chalk** removes grease stains
- use **peanut butter** to remove scuff marks from sneakers
- put **meat tenderizer** (enzymes such as bromelain, which can be bought in grocery shops) on sweaty armpit stains before washing
- finally, if you need to do this, **coffee grounds** remove vomit (and the smell)

Next: Dry cleaning →

Dry cleaning: because you can't launder everything

Watch for those little symbols! (A) (P) ⊠

What happens at the cleaners

1 SPOTTING

Depending on what marks are on your clothes, specialised **spotting agents** are applied by hand. They remove or loosen the stains.

2 WASHING

Your clothes do get wet, but with **solvents,** not water. The solvent most commonly used in dry cleaning is known as **perc*.** It acts on clothes in a similar manner to mineral spirits cleaning a paint brush.

wet cycle
12 minutes

Since solvents are considered hazardous wastes, they cannot be dumped down the drain after use. Instead, they must be **recycled** through filtration or distillation.

That dry-cleaning smell can mean that the perc isn't being recycled as thoroughly as it should be.

*Perc is the common name for perchloroethylene (tetrachloroethylene).

3 DRYING

This is done in the same machine as the wash.

dry cycle
35 minutes

Hey! where are my spots?

Weather guru

Weather sayings are often based on local observations, not science, so they may not apply in different parts of the world. Nevertheless we repeat them endlessly. So here are some that seem to be fairly accurate weather forecasters.

" When the glass falls low, prepare for a blow. When it rises high, let all your kites fly. "

The "glass" refers to the mercury in a glass barometer. When barometric pressure falls, a low pressure weather system is developing or moving nearer. **Wind, clouds and storms are associated with low pressure.**

Conversely **rising pressure means the weather is clearing.** "Let all your kites fly" really means it's going to be a nice day to go outside to play, not that it'll be especially windy.

" Red sky in the morning, shepherds' warning; red sky at night, shepherds' delight. *"

But *why*? The explanation is a bit complicated. Here goes:

Storm systems basically move from west to east. **A red sky in the morning** implies that the rising sun is shining on clouds to the west, and conditions to the east are clear. Clouds moving in from the west mean a weather system is approaching. Be warned!

A red sky in the evening implies that the setting sun is shining on clouds in the east, which are moving away—further east. That means better weather. Be delighted!

" A year of snow, a year of plenty. "

Continuous snow cover on orchards and farms delays the blossoming of fruit trees until frosty days and nights are over. It also prevents freezing and thawing cycles that can destroy wheat and other crops.

*Some say sailors instead of shepherds.

> **A rainbow in the morning gives you warning.**
With the sun in the east, the rain and its rainbow are in the west. Since weather moves from west to east, **a morning rainbow means that the rain is coming towards you.**

> **If the rooster crows on going to bed, you may rise with a watery head.**
I have no idea why. But farmer Jones swears by this one.

> **When the stars begin to huddle, the earth will soon be a puddle.**
This is just an optical illusion: when clouds increase, whole areas of stars in the night sky are hidden. In the remaining open areas, stars appear to huddle together. **More clouds means a greater chance of rain.**

Nature: the best forecaster?

In order not to have their pollen washed away, **flowers** close up as humidity rises.

Cicadas cannot vibrate their wings when humidity is high, so they may be silent when rain is approaching.

The higher the humidity, the better sound travels.
In England, people used to estimate the chance of rain by how clearly they could hear the ringing of church bells.

A drop in barometric pressure can affect the digestive system of **COWS,** meaning they don't feel like grazing, but instead lie down. (If it rains, it does keep the ground dry under them, but that's not why they do it.)

Motorcyclist

Whether you're after a job as a motorcycle messenger or just want have fun riding around with a friend, you need to know some basic truths.

Number one: **motorbikes are dangerous!**

It's a babe magnet!
Beware: after a couple of rides on the back, she'll want to drive your bike too.

It's heavy!
Make sure it doesn't fall over. It'll hurt if you are under it. A lot.

It's powerful!
Be careful when you turn up the gas. The front wheel can easily lift off. Daredevils will do "wheelies" on purpose, but it's not recommended if you want to get home safely for a nice cup of tea.

If you only remember one thing, it's this:

When you're on the road, **imagine you are invisible.** Car drivers often cannot, or do not, see you.

Wear these

- A good all-over helmet with moveable visor. (And please get one for passengers, too.)

- Heavy jacket with padded chest, back and elbows. (Some jackets even have metal inserts for ultimate protection. Those are *really* heavy.)

- Padded gloves.

- Proper boots—and never sneakers or flip-flops.

Next: Signals ➜

Bikers' sign language

Seven of the signals a leader makes to riders behind. All made with the left hand.

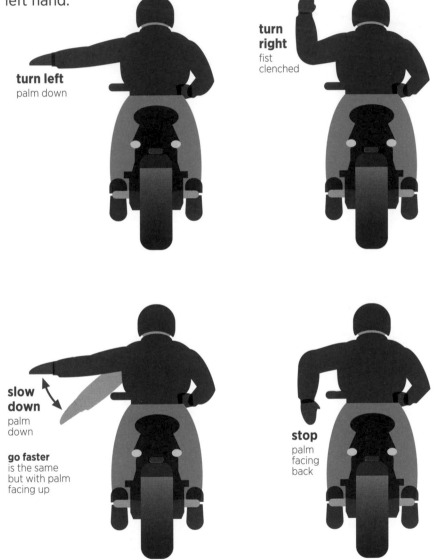

turn left
palm down

turn right
fist clenched

slow down
palm down

go faster
is the same but with palm facing up

stop
palm facing back

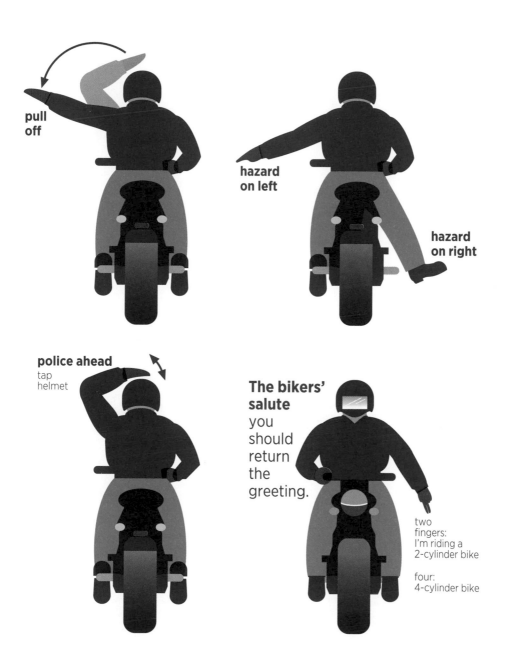

pull off

hazard on left

hazard on right

police ahead
tap helmet

The bikers' salute
you should return the greeting.

two fingers: I'm riding a 2-cylinder bike

four: 4-cylinder bike

Concierge

A good hotel concierge is the **gatekeeper of the city.** He (or she) knows the top maitre d's, the hard-to-get ticket sources, the finest tailors—the best, most opulent things their town has to offer.

How may I be of help?

ANY QUESTIONS?

Whether it's a simple request, such as finding the best parking spot or an almost impossible one, like arranging the aquisition and overseas shipping of an authentic London double-decker bus, it all comes down to the **address book.**

GOOD ANSWERS

But it's not just knowing the right people; a concierge must be quite the **know-it-all.*** When asked about the best bottle of whisky that money can buy, the concierge must be a single malt connoisseur. A guest wants to rent a fast, luxury sports car? The good concierge knows the latest models and where they are available **beyond the usual** well-known rental-car companies.

AN EXCLUSIVE CLUB

If you want to become a member of the prestigious French association **Les Clefs d'Or** (Golden Keys), you'll need at least five years' experience in the hotel industry, plus the backing of two current members, before going before a rigorous board review. There are only 3,500 members, worldwide.

Sight-
seeing

Con
prior

Greater
thread
count

Drinks
on the roof
at midnight

*Seems like this book should be required reading for all concierges!

Airline upgrades

Last-minute tickets

Special rentals

Exclusive travel plans

Difficult reservations

he ...est spot ...n the ...each

A pet's special birthday

That's a busy brain! (For a different take on honeycomb, see *How to be a Beekeeper*.)

ORGANISING PRINCIPLES
With many customers to please— almost all of whom probably count themselves as rather more important than anyone else nearby— a concierge (that's you!) must be **highly organised** in taking care of several unusual and time-sensitive requests all at once.

THE CUSTOMER IS ALWAYS...
impatient. You must return to your customers with **solutions, not problems.** Being able to make a quick decision to fulfill the needs of the rich and entitled is a big plus.

A MODEL OF DISCRETION
As a conscientious concierge, you should never break the law for a guest. Pushing the law is a bit different. A rich customer will pay generously for your discretion. **Keep your eyes open and your mouth firmly closed!**

HOW TO START
Some universities offer courses in hospitality, and some hotels provide formal training themselves, most people learn on the job.

ONLY IN HOTELS?
No. There's a growing field of **personal concierge services.** Among them: pet-sitting, event planning, waiting in line, general housekeeping. Have a look at *How to be a Butler* too.

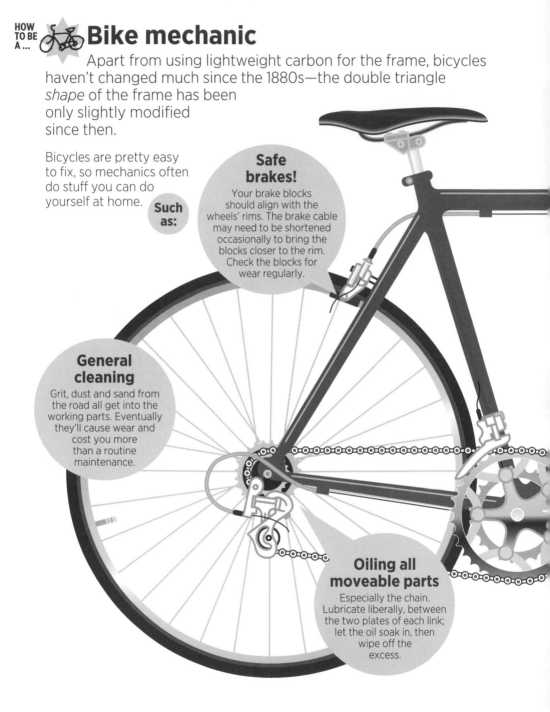

Bike mechanic

Apart from using lightweight carbon for the frame, bicycles haven't changed much since the 1880s—the double triangle *shape* of the frame has been only slightly modified since then.

Bicycles are pretty easy to fix, so mechanics often do stuff you can do yourself at home. **Such as:**

Safe brakes!
Your brake blocks should align with the wheels' rims. The brake cable may need to be shortened occasionally to bring the blocks closer to the rim. Check the blocks for wear regularly.

General cleaning
Grit, dust and sand from the road all get into the working parts. Eventually they'll cause wear and cost you more than a routine maintenance.

Oiling all moveable parts
Especially the chain. Lubricate liberally, between the two plates of each link; let the oil soak in, then wipe off the excess.

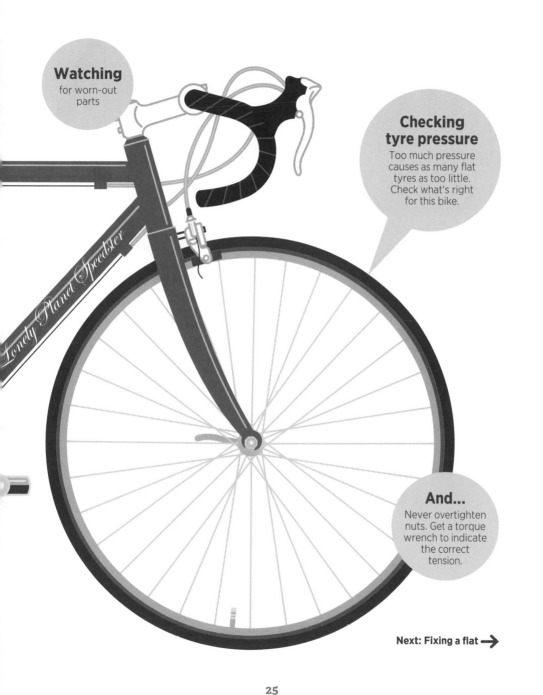

Watching
for worn-out parts

Checking tyre pressure
Too much pressure causes as many flat tyres as too little. Check what's right for this bike.

And...
Never overtighten nuts. Get a torque wrench to indicate the correct tension.

Next: Fixing a flat →

Fixing a flat

Not that difficult. You can do it!

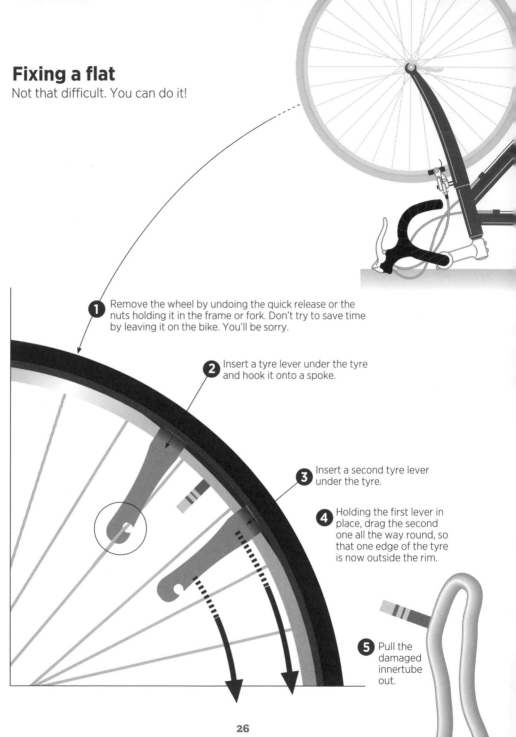

1 Remove the wheel by undoing the quick release or the nuts holding it in the frame or fork. Don't try to save time by leaving it on the bike. You'll be sorry.

2 Insert a tyre lever under the tyre and hook it onto a spoke.

3 Insert a second tyre lever under the tyre.

4 Holding the first lever in place, drag the second one all the way round, so that one edge of the tyre is now outside the rim.

5 Pull the damaged innertube out.

6 Run your fingers around the inside of the empty tyre for anything (a nail? tack? piece of glass?) that might have caused the flat. Careful: perhaps wear a glove.

7 Slightly inflate a new innertube.

8 Poke the valve on this new innertube through the wheel's valve hole, and feed the innertube into the tyre all the way round.

9 Push the open edge of the tyre into the rim, and make sure the tyre is seated properly in the wheel.

10 Pump it up! Follow the tyre manufacturer's recommended pressure (see previous page). And be sure you know a Presta valve from a Schrader valve.

Presta

Schrader

Flight attendant

If you think passengers would never dare to physically poke attendants to get attention, clip their toenails mid flight, or try to join the mile high club, think again! Airline crew need to have a thick skin, the patience of a saint, and a good sense of humour.

A LIFE IN THE AIR
'Routine' is not a common word in a flight attendant's lexicon. With long, unpredictable hours, flight delays and the difficulties of living out of a bag miles and miles from home, this is a job for the adventurous spirit.

PEOPLE MANAGEMENT
A flight attendant should be friendly and approachable, with the ability to listen to passengers' concerns and anticipate their needs.

SAFETY FIRST
Flight attendants must be able to recite the emergency procedures by heart, and go through the pre-flight safety demo even though they can see that few are listening.*

Sorry, I pressed the overhead call button by mistake.

Why is the plane ALWAYS delayed?

I need another drink! NOW.

Hic!

Yes, I *know* how to insert the buckle ...

They have to say it.

*At initiation ceremonies for trainees, colleagues in the back of the plane try to make them laugh.

ATTENDANTS' FLIGHT TIPS

To beat jetlag, drink lots of water, a little at a time.

Pack healthy snacks: veggies! fruit!

Pack mini toiletries and spare underwear in your carry-on luggage. Then if your checked luggage is lost, you can still get through a day without being too stinky.

DO YOU SPEAK AIRLINE FOOD?

Most airlines require at least a reasonable fluency in another language.

Voici votre repas.

Et puis-je avoir de l'eau, s'il vous plaît?

Oui, bien sur!

LET'S GET PHYSICAL

The job isn't all about demeanour. A flight attendant (male or female) must be between 1.5m (5ft 2in) and 1.8m (6ft 2in) tall, with their weight in proportion to their height. They also need good vision, and cannot be colour blind.

Be prepared to negotiate traffic jams in the overhead bins.

No male attendants on this fight, eh?

So?

Final fun fact: Some airlines don't allow tattoos or body piercings.

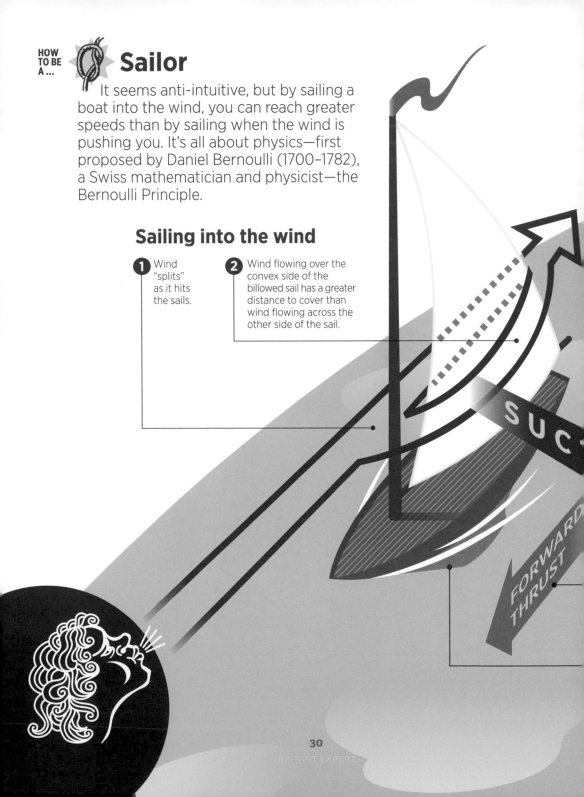

Sailor

It seems anti-intuitive, but by sailing a boat into the wind, you can reach greater speeds than by sailing when the wind is pushing you. It's all about physics—first proposed by Daniel Bernoulli (1700–1782), a Swiss mathematician and physicist—the Bernoulli Principle.

Sailing into the wind

1 Wind "splits" as it hits the sails.

2 Wind flowing over the convex side of the billowed sail has a greater distance to cover than wind flowing across the other side of the sail.

SUC...

FORWARD THRUST

Avast there, mateys!* In my day, sailors got scurvy. Make sure you've got oranges (or vitamin C pills) on board if you plan a long trip!*

* September 19 is International Talk Like a Pirate day. Really. It was started in 1995 by John Baur and Mark Summers.

3 The unequal flow of air across the two sides of the sail produces a powerful **suction,** similar to the lifting force that results from air flowing over an aircraft wing. This is what's called the Bernoulli Principle.

HEELING FORCE

4 Suction comprises a **heeling force** and a **forward thrust.**

5 The boat's **keel** counteracts the sideways push of the heeling force, channelling the energy into forward motion.

2 basic manoeuvres

Tacking is when you zigzag against the wind. (You can't sail *directly* into the wind.)

TACK TACK

TACK

JIBE

JIBE JIBE

Jibing happens when the wind is blowing from behind you. As the boat turns the wind forces the sail to swing across the deck quickly. This is where you should **duck!**

Next: Knots →

31

Tying knots

Knowing knots is one of the first skills you need to make your boat secure, whether it's in dock or on the open water. Here are some of the basic knots, hitches and bends you should know. Practise with a bit of thick string.

QUICK GLOSSARY

Knot, hitch and bend are often used interchangeably, but their different definitions are useful.

A **knot,** when tied, remains a knot ...

... while a **hitch** is a knot tied around an object, and when the object is removed, the knot falls apart.

A **bend** is used to join the ends of two ropes together, like these two.

Sheet Bend
Used to join two ropes together.

Reef Knot
A simple way to tie the two ends of a rope together.
It also can be used as a bend to join two ropes.

WHEN A ROPE IS NOT A ROPE?

In sailing, a **rope** is called a **line,** unless it's part of the sail's rigging, where it's called a **sheet**. Got that?

Sailor's Knot
A secure way to attach a rope to an object.
But it's not a hitch because it remains a knot without the object.

Stevedore's Knot
When pulled tight, this makes a good stopper at the end of a rope.

Overhand Knot
The most basic of all knots. It's frequently used to make other knots and hitches.

Figure Eight Knot
(Also called: Flemish Knot; Savoy Knot)
The standard maritime knot, it can also be used as a decorative feature.

Lark's Head
Used to attach a rope to a ring or other object.

Clove Hitch
Used to tie a rope around an object.

Bowline
Use this to make a fixed loop at the end of a rope.
Two of these loops on one rope can be used to lift a person.

Timber Hitch
Used to attach a rope to a post or other object.

Lariat Loop
Commonly used on a lasso.
When there's a bull running wild on your boat, use this. Hey, you never know.

Slip Knot
(Also: Running Knot)
Attaches a rope to an object, closing around it when pulled tight.
The knot used by hangmen in America's Wild West.

Next: Oops, and anchors →

Oops!

You're bound to capsize sometime, so here's how to right a small boat, and get back in.

1

2

Finally ...

how to drop anchor

1

Lower sails and roll them up.

2

Find a spot 30m (100ft) from other boats, and away from cliffs and sea walls, etc.

3

Turn the boat to **face the wind** or current.

Yachtsman's anchor

4

Slowly **lower the anchor** over the bow until it reaches the bottom.

Fluke anchor

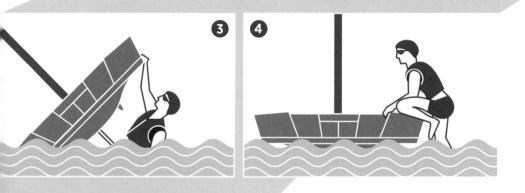

5 If you have an **engine (or outboard motor), set it in reverse** and and move **slowly** away from the anchor until it bites.

6 Tie the rope (line) around the cleat with a **cleat hitch.**

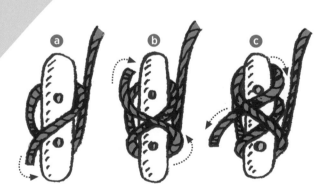

Swimmer

Well, you probably do know how to swim, but this will help you to be a better, faster **aquatic athlete.** (And you can call yourself that when you want to show off.)

1 **Kick efficiently: don't let your feet rise above the water line**

This maximises the effort you put into kicking, and minimises drag. (see 2, below.)

2 **Streamline your body to decrease drag**

You can do this by keeping the body horizontal in the water, and not letting your backside and legs drift downwards. This is called balancing the body.

3 **Instead of swimming on your stomach, roll from side to side with each stroke**

By doing this you'll be presenting a slimmer profile and less resistance to the water, enabling you to glide through it like a fish. And you'll be using the core muscles of your back, hips and torso to apply more force to the stroke.

4 Swim "taller"

Using the principle that a longer, tapered vessel glides through water more easily and faster than a shorter one, reach out as far as you can with each stroke, and leave your hand there longer before retracting to start the next stroke.

5 Keep your head and eyes down

Bringing your head up works against the effort of keeping the body in a straight line—it unbalances you.

6 OK, so you have to breathe!

Raise your head slightly, when you have rolled to one side or the other, to grab a quick breath.

7 Keep your fingers slightly open ...

not tight together nor wide apart. A separation actually makes a web of water between the fingers, giving you more "pull."

Lifeguard

You are already a sun and sand addict. Now you want to be part beach police officer and part paramedic.

Yes? Well, you must:

① be a strong swimmer!

② be trained in first aid and lifesaving techniques, including CPR.

③ able to confidently enforce beach rules.

④ concentrate for long periods (when nothing seems to be happening).

⑤ anticipate potential problems.

⑥ act quickly in an emergency.

And you'll need:

- whistle
- flotation device
- high lookout seat

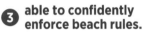
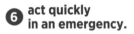

- 3m (10ft) rescue board

Whistle while you work

 One short blast
to get the attention of a swimmer

 Two short blasts
to get the attention of
fellow lifeguards

 **Three short blasts**
to get the attention of
fellow lifeguards and let them
know an emergency is happening

 **One long blast**
to get everyone out of the water

Beach safety flags

Danger or hazard
no swimming

On some beaches,
two red flags means
Danger no swimming

Caution
seek advice

**Safe
to swim**

**Lifeguard
on duty**

Surfing area
no swimming

**Scuba diving
in progress**
keep well clear

An
alternate
flotation
device,
called a
"rescue can"

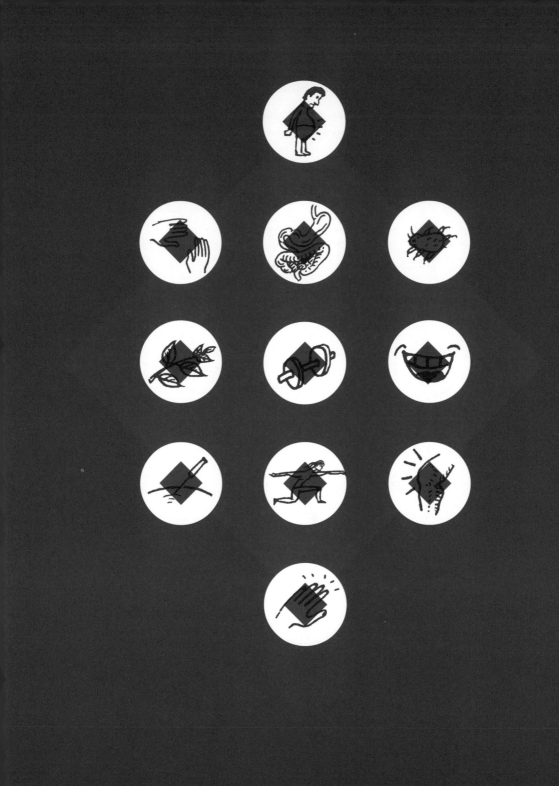

HEALTH

Nutritionist

While explaining the importance of nutrients, nutritionists are also searching for ways to understand the world's obesity epidemic. (It's approaching the number one killer disease.)

There are many theories about how to lose weight.* All of them involve **metabolism.**

Metabolism encompasses a multitude of chemical changes in which food either builds and repairs cells, or is converted into energy.

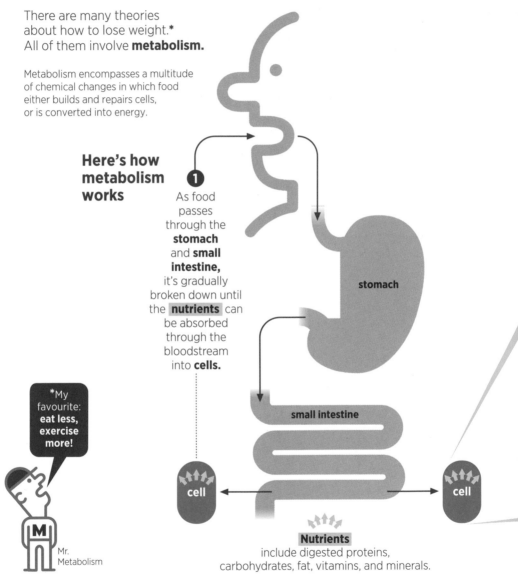

Here's how metabolism works

1 As food passes through the **stomach** and **small intestine,** it's gradually broken down until the **nutrients** can be absorbed through the bloodstream into **cells.**

stomach

small intestine

*My favourite: **eat less, exercise more!**

Mr. Metabolism

cell

cell

Nutrients include digested proteins, carbohydrates, fat, vitamins, and minerals.

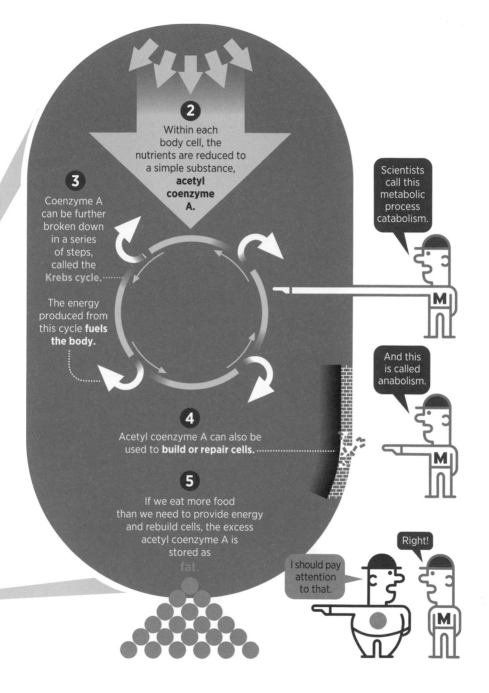

 # Masseur

A masseur, or masseuse, applies pressure to a client's muscles and connective tissue, normally using hands and fingers (and less often, with elbows, knees or forearms).

What does massage do?

- **relieves muscle pain**
- **relieves mental anxiety**
- **reduces blood pressure and heart rate**
- **restores energy**
- **provides feelings of calm and relaxation**

Turn down the lights

Naked? Only if the client feels comfortable with that.

The face rests comfortably in a horseshoe-shaped padded ring.

⬭ Oils

Use all sorts including:

- **almond**
- **coconut**
- **grape seed**
- **jojoba**
- **olive**
- **pecan**
- **macadamia**
- **sesame**
- **baby oil**
- or a mixture!

Play some soft music.

What makes a good masseur?

- Friendly table-side manner
- A thorough knowledge of anatomy and physiology
- Strong hands (and a strong physique: it's exhausting work)
- Good intuitition and the confidence to know how to help the client
- Having a fast laundry service!

Different types

These are the most popular:

- **accupressure** — a traditional Chinese method; pressure is applied to acupuncture points
- **craniosacral** — light touches to the skull, face, spine and pelvis relieve tension
- **hot stone massage** — smooth, water-heated rocks apply pressure and heat
- **reflexology** — massaging hands and feet; reflexes there relate to every system in the body
- **reiki*** — hand and palm strokes are used to relieve ailments
- **shiatsu*** — finger and palm pressure
- **Swedish** — the classic treatment; long flowing strokes
- **Thai massage** — deep full-body massage applied from the feet up

*While popular, these are not shown to have much medical benefit.

The padded table top is lined with a clean sheet.

Mobile masseurs use folding tables to treat people in their homes or offices. (Warning: the tables are not that light!)

Do you have to be licensed to practice?

Yes and no. Here's a selection of regulations from around the world.

- **China** massage mostly unregulated
- **France** 3 years of study followed by two exams
- **Germany** 3,200 hours of training
- **India** licensed by the Ministry of Health
- **Japan** shiatsu is licensed, but Thai massage is not, nor is the use of oil
- **New Zealand** unregulated
- **UK** unregulated
- **US** 500–1,000 hours of training (there are about 300,000 massage therapists and students in the US)

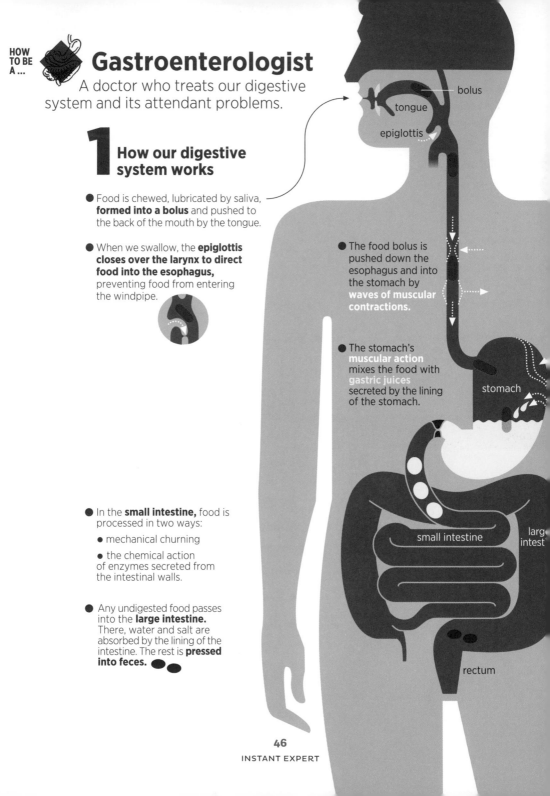

Gastroenterologist

A doctor who treats our digestive system and its attendant problems.

1 How our digestive system works

- Food is chewed, lubricated by saliva, **formed into a bolus** and pushed to the back of the mouth by the tongue.

- When we swallow, the **epiglottis closes over the larynx to direct food into the esophagus,** preventing food from entering the windpipe.

- The food bolus is pushed down the esophagus and into the stomach by **waves of muscular contractions.**

- The stomach's **muscular action** mixes the food with gastric juices secreted by the lining of the stomach.

- In the **small intestine,** food is processed in two ways:
  - mechanical churning
  - the chemical action of enzymes secreted from the intestinal walls.

- Any undigested food passes into the **large intestine.** There, water and salt are absorbed by the lining of the intestine. The rest is **pressed into feces.**

bolus

tongue

epiglottis

stomach

small intestine

larg intest

rectum

Some of the problems a gastroenterologist treats

(Note: It'll take you a minimum of 13 years of school and training before you can qualify to treat patients!)

> **difficulty swallowing**

> **frequent nausea**

> **heartburn, acid reflux and GERD**
> (gastroesophageal reflux disease)

> **hiatal hernias**

> **ulcers** →

> **cancers**
> (mostly stomach, but gastroenterologists also treat biliary system organs: liver cancer, pancreatic cancer)

> **general abdominal pain**

> **bleeding in the digestive tract**

> **colon diseases**
> (diverticulitis, Crohn's, irritable bowel syndrome,)

> **colorectal cancer** →
> This is one of the most common cancers, affecting both men and women. A colonoscopy allows a gastroenterologist to insert a **scope** to see and remove small polyps that could become cancerous.

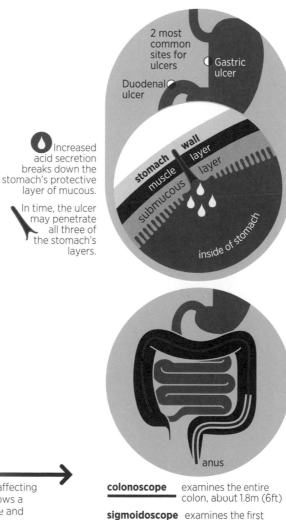

2 most common sites for ulcers

Gastric ulcer

Duodenal ulcer

Increased acid secretion breaks down the stomach's protective layer of mucous.

In time, the ulcer may penetrate all three of the stomach's layers.

stomach wall
muscle layer
submucous layer
inside of stomach

anus

colonoscope — examines the entire colon, about 1.8m (6ft)

sigmoidoscope — examines the first 28cm (11in) of the colon

Parasitologist

Parasites are scary to look at and do scary things to us.
A parasitologist studies ways to treat diseases caused by parasites, by
developing drugs. **Travellers: know your enemies!**

**Humans are hosts to 300 species of parasitic worms
and 70 species of protozoa that are invisible to our eyes.**
Being a host means that these organisms can live
on or inside us.* Here are four of the nasty little things.

(Actually,
the tapeworm
isn't so little.)

Plasmodium

How does it get into you?
Mosquito bites

What does it cause? Malaria

Where is it prevalent? 97 countries,
including sub-Saharan Africa, India,
China, Brazil and most of SE Asia.
An estimated 627,000 people died
of malaria in 2012.

Giardia

**How does it
get into you?**
Contaminated water
and food; contact
with a person
who has giardiasis.

What does it cause?
Dysentery, diarrhoea

Where is it prevalent?
Worldwide**

*Endoparasites live inside
us; ectoparasites live
"outside"—but just under
the skin, like the tick on
the next page.

** Every continent except Antarctica

Tapeworms in humans can reach an incredible 15.3m (55ft)

Tapeworm

How does it get into you?
Undercooked, infected food

What does it cause?
Often there are no serious symptoms. A sign of infection may be segments of the worms when you poop.

Where is it prevalent?
Worldwide** (mostly in underdeveloped countries)

Scapularis (deer) tick

How does it get into you?
Ticks attach themselves to bare arms or legs. While sucking your blood, they introduce infection to the blood stream.

What does it cause? Lyme disease

Where is it prevalent? Worldwide**

Good luck finding them—this is the actual size.

There's little time after a bite and before the disease develops, so it's important to check your arms and legs after walking in fields or woods where deer are known to live. Make sure you remove the whole tick with tweezers. If infected, some people develop a bull's-eye rash.

HOW
TO BE
A ...

Naturopath

Naturopathy is the treatment of illness by studying underlying causes rather than symptoms. The naturopathic doctor teaches patients to be responsible for their own health—it's easier to prevent a disease than to treat one.

- Advocating a healthy attitude, lifestyle and diet are part of the treatment, as are certain natural extracts.

- **Here are some of the most popular botanicals.**
  (And where you can gather them)

Garlic
to lower cholesterol
(widely available)

Cranberry
for urinary tract problems
(North America)

St. John's Wort
for menopause
(widely available)

Black Cohosh
for menopause
(North America)

Soy
for menopause
(North America, Brazil, Argentina, China, India)

Note: many studies have been done on the effectiveness of these supplements and naturopathic medicine as a whole. Not all of them have been complimentary.

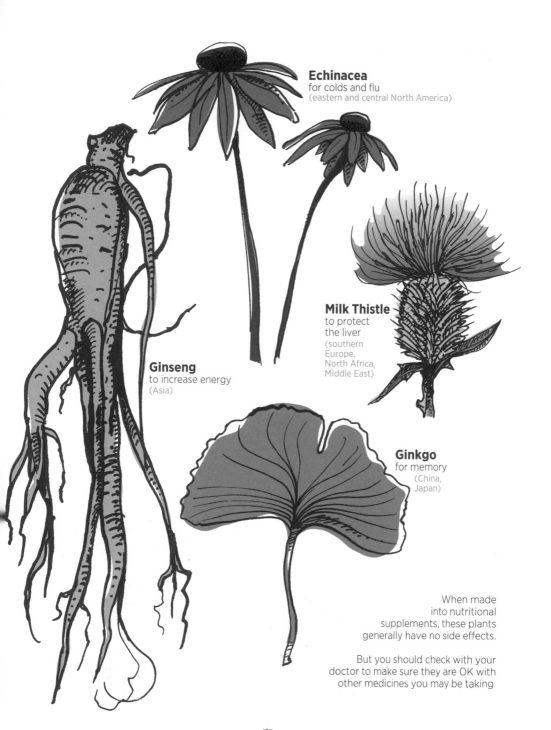

Echinacea
for colds and flu
(eastern and central North America)

Milk Thistle
to protect
the liver
(southern
Europe,
North Africa,
Middle East)

Ginseng
to increase energy
(Asia)

Ginkgo
for memory
(China,
Japan)

When made
into nutritional
supplements, these plants
generally have no side effects.

But you should check with your
doctor to make sure they are OK with
other medicines you may be taking.

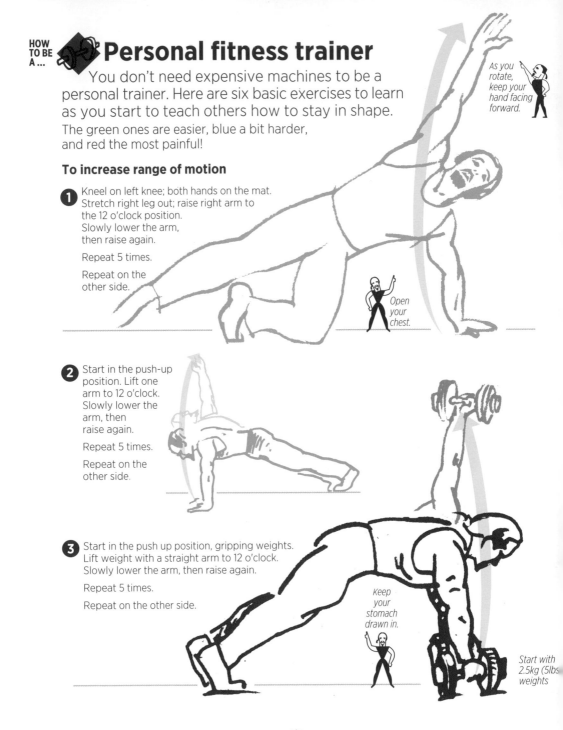

Personal fitness trainer

HOW TO BE A ...

You don't need expensive machines to be a personal trainer. Here are six basic exercises to learn as you start to teach others how to stay in shape.

The green ones are easier, blue a bit harder, and red the most painful!

As you rotate, keep your hand facing forward.

To increase range of motion

1 Kneel on left knee; both hands on the mat. Stretch right leg out; raise right arm to the 12 o'clock position. Slowly lower the arm, then raise again.

Repeat 5 times.

Repeat on the other side.

Open your chest.

2 Start in the push-up position. Lift one arm to 12 o'clock. Slowly lower the arm, then raise again.

Repeat 5 times.

Repeat on the other side.

3 Start in the push up position, gripping weights. Lift weight with a straight arm to 12 o'clock. Slowly lower the arm, then raise again.

Repeat 5 times.

Repeat on the other side.

Keep your stomach drawn in.

Start with 2.5kg (5lbs weights

52

INSTANT EXPERT

To strengthen torso and hips

4 Lie on your back with knees bent and hands on hips. Push hips up, tilting them backwards as you lift yourself up to the horizontal position.

Repeat 10 times.

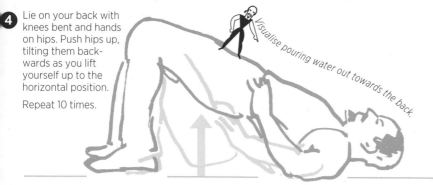

Visualise pouring water out towards the back.

5 Place yourself on the ball. Lower hips slowly (a), tilt pelvis, then lift up (b).

Repeat 10 times.

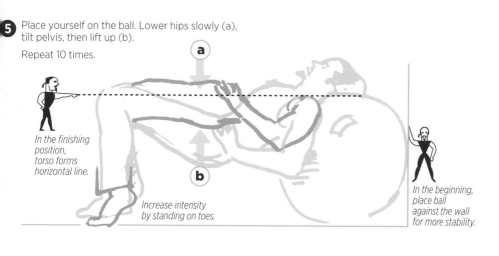

a

b

In the finishing position, torso forms horizontal line.

Increase intensity by standing on toes.

In the beginning, place ball against the wall for more stability.

6 Same position as before, but use weights for extra resistance.

Start with 4.5kg (10lbs)

Exercise balls are slightly squishy, inflated rubber spheres. They come in various sizes.

Emergency dentist

Your teeth are pretty strong, but accidents happen. Here's how to alleviate some of the pain (and possible infection) when you break a tooth. But you should see a real dentist quickly!

1 **There are three different levels of damage:**

- **chip** } more
- **break** } serious

When a large piece of tooth breaks off, the nerve may be exposed. → Exposure to saliva, air or hold or cold food can cause real pain.

- **fracture** You might not notice a minor crack at first. But later, you may feel pain if the damage extends to the nerve, or when you put pressure on the tooth when chewing food.

— enamel
— dentin
— pulp
— nerves

2 **Keep the broken piece if you can.** Pay attention when you are eating nuts: they are a big culprit! Don't swallow if you sense a problem; spit it all out. (Apologise if you are with others.)

3rd molar (wisdom)

2nd molar

1st molar

IN THE MOUTH ↗
What you can do for yourself or others

premolar

premolar

canine

incisor

inc

BELOW
What a dentist can do for you ↓

⚑ **Filling** is for small breaks.

⚑ **Bonding** fits a resin copy of the tooth over the broken piece.

⚑ **Crowns or caps** are used for bigger breaks. The dentist files the broken tooth down and "caps" it with a model of the whole tooth.

⚑ **Veneers**—porcelain or resin slip covers—are usually fitted to front teeth.

⚑ **Root canals** are needed when the pulp of the tooth is damaged and opened up to possible infection. After cleaning, the tooth is capped. This one hurts!

**Take a painkiller
if necessary.**
An over-the-counter
non-steroidal anti-
inflammatory drug
(NSAID) such as
ibuprofen, or a pain
medicine such as
acetaminophen will
help until a dentist
prescribes something
stronger.

**Cover jagged or sharp
tooth edges with
paraffin wax.**
If you don't have any
paraffin wax (I know I
don't!) use sugarless
chewing gum instead.
If you can't reach a
dentist but can get to a
chemist, buy temporary
dental cement, and cover
the tooth with that.

paraffin wax / sugarless chewing gum
or temporary dental cement

**Rinse your mouth,
then gargle with
salt water.**
This'll help stop
possible infection.

**Use a cold compress
to reduce swelling
and pain.**
This will make you more
comfortable if you have
to wait for treatment.

(A cold compress is a
pad of material soaked
in ice-cold water and held in place
with a bandage, or just your hand.)

If you must, take another
painkiller, but never exceed
the recommended
dosage.

**To stop bleeding,
hold a pad of gauze
(or bunched up
tissue) to the broken
tooth for 10 minutes.**
If this doesn't work,
rinse your mouth with
cold water. (The cold
will contract blood
vessels.)

← same as the other side! →

REMEMBER
You should **see a dentist** whenever you feel
sensitivity in your mouth, especially when you
are eating or from changes in temperature.
Pain is an indication that a break or fracture
may have damaged the nerve or the pulp
(see cross-section above) in your tooth.

Acupunturist

Wanna stick needles into other people? Acupuncture is the thing for you! You'll be practising a very old traditional form of Chinese medicine, which holds that there's an energy force running through the body, called **Qi.** (It's pronounced "chee", a good word to remember for Scrabble.)

The basics

1 **Qi** is carried through the body by a network of channels, or meridians (●━●━●). Ailments arise when these meridians become blocked.

2 You insert **really thin needles** at specific trigger points along the meridians to help adjust the flow and balance of Qi.

3 Western medicine suggests that the needles send messages to the brain, which in turn releases pain-killing **endorphins.**

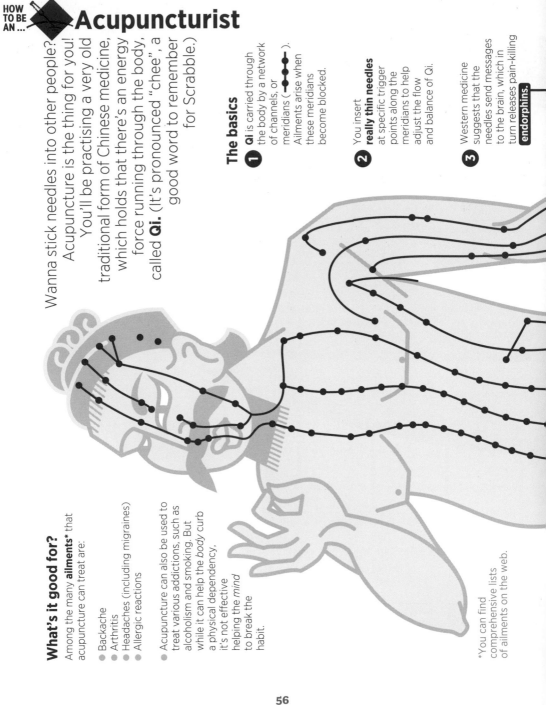

What's it good for?

Among the many **ailments*** that acupuncture can treat are:

- Backache
- Arthritis
- Headaches (including migraines)
- Allergic reactions

- Acupuncture can also be used to treat various addictions, such as alcoholism and smoking. But while it can help the *body* curb a physical dependency, it's not effective helping the *mind* to break the habit.

*You can find comprehensive lists of ailments on the web.

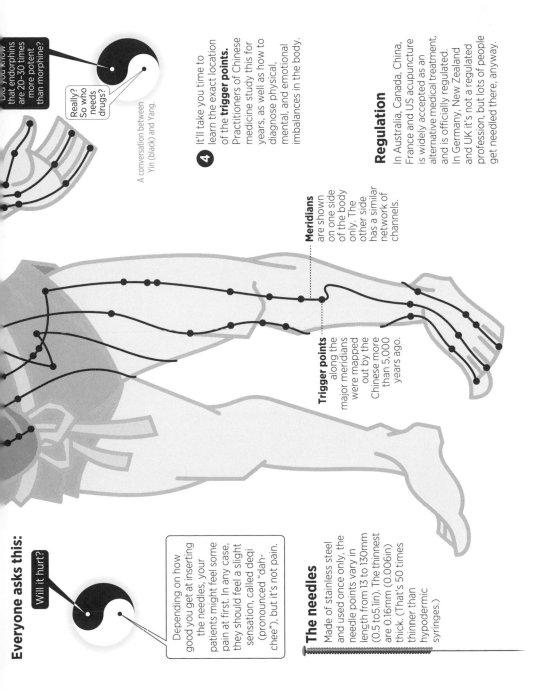

Did you know that endorphins are 20-30 times more potent than morphine?

Really? So who needs drugs?

A conversation between Yin (black) and Yang.

4 It'll take you time to learn the exact location of the **trigger points.** Practitioners of Chinese medicine study this for years, as well as how to diagnose physical, mental, and emotional imbalances in the body.

Regulation

In Australia, Canada, China, France and US acupuncture is widely accepted as an alternative medical treatment, and is officially regulated. In Germany, New Zealand and UK it's not a regulated profession, but lots of people get needled there, anyway.

Meridians are shown on one side of the body only. The other side has a similar network of channels.

Trigger points along the major meridians were mapped out by the Chinese more than 5,000 years ago.

Everyone asks this:

Will it hurt?

Depending on how good you get at inserting the needles, your patients might feel some pain at first. In any case, they should feel a slight sensation, called deqi (pronounced "dah-chee"), but it's not pain.

The needles

Made of stainless steel and used once only, the needle points vary in length from 13 to 130mm (0.5 to5.1in). The thinnest are 0.16mm (0.006in) thick. (That's 50 times thinner than hypodermic syringes.)

Yogi

Yoga is old: 5,000 year-old stone figures in yogic poses have been found in the Indus valley (modern-day Pakistan-India).

There are many forms, or schools, of yoga. In some, like Bikram, the temperature of the room is raised to 40°C (105°F), but most are based on a set of poses, called *asanas*. **Here are some of the most basic poses.**

The Sun Salutation sequence
Often the first thing in a yoga session. (Try it outdoors

The Bridge

The Bow

The Crow

The Shoulder Stand

The Plough

This one is the Cobra pose

And this, Downward Dog

The Triangle

The Tree

The Warrior

Five yoga principles

Exercises, like those shown here stretch and tone muscles and ligaments.

Proper **breathing** uses your entire lungs to increase oxygen intake.

A well-balanced and nourishing **diet** keeps the body fit and resistant to disease.

Positive thinking removes harmful negative thoughts.

Relaxation releases tension in muscles and calms the mind.

Arthroscopic surgeon

Let's hope you don't twist your knee while climbing up the Eiffel Tower or down the Grand Canyon or, more likely, playing a casual game of football in the park.

But if you do, you'll need the attention of a good arthroscopic surgeon.

Arthroscopy is minimally invasive surgery — typically used on a damaged joint.

Its advantages include:
- joints don't have to be fully opened up
- recovery time is reduced
- there's less scarring

Ouch!

Knees are built to **bend, hinge-like, not rotate.** So a sudden twist on the football field can damage the knee joint.

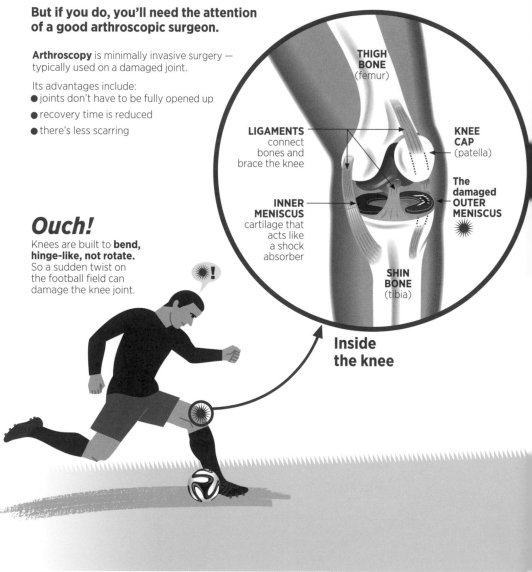

THIGH BONE (femur)

LIGAMENTS connect bones and brace the knee

KNEE CAP (patella)

The damaged OUTER MENISCUS

INNER MENISCUS cartilage that acts like a shock absorber

SHIN BONE (tibia)

Inside the knee

How you use an arthroscope to repair torn cartilage.

(*Meniscus* is just a surgeon's word for it. You'll seem smarter if you use different words.)

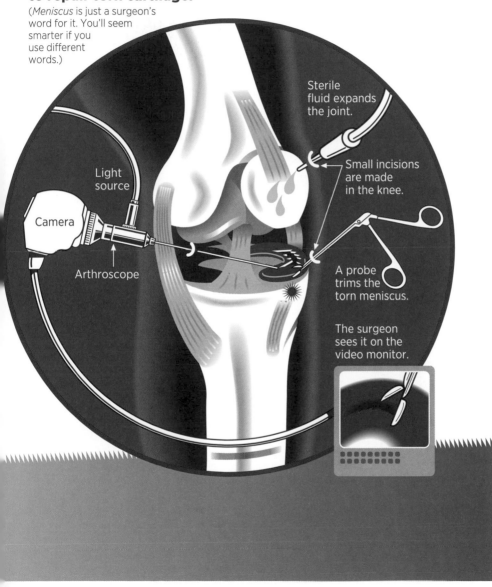

Sterile fluid expands the joint.

Small incisions are made in the knee.

Light source

Camera

Arthroscope

A probe trims the torn meniscus.

The surgeon sees it on the video monitor.

Manicurist

A manicurist cleans, cuts, files, paints and polishes fingernails.

(A pedicurist does the same for toes, plus she (or he) treats corns and callouses.)

Essential Equipment

For a basic, unisex* manicure you'll need:

- Cotton balls or cotton swabs
- Cuticle trimmer
- Nail buffer
- Nail file
- Cuticle or hand cream
- Nail clippers

Step-by-step

❶ Cut and file the nails

- Start with the nail clippers. Ask your manicure client to rest their hand in front of you on a hand towel.

- Finger by finger, gently trim each nail. Don't cut them too short! Make sure some of the white edge of the nail remains visible.

- Then take the file and carefully file away the rough edges of the nail, creating a smooth curve as you go.

❷ Get buff

- Polish each nail with the buffer, gently rubbing back and forth to make the surface as smooth as you can.

❸ Soak and clean

- Place the hand in a bowl of water so that the nails are submerged.

- Leave for a couple of minutes, then take a nail brush and clean any dirt from beneath the nails.

*This is a unisex thing? That hand looks pretty feminine.

So? Would you rather have seen a man's hand?

4 Cuticle correction

- You can use some cuticle cream, or maybe hand lotion if that's ... handy.
- Rub some cream into the finger nails and surrounding skin.
- Take the cuticle trimmer and gently push the cuticle (the thin layer of skin that grows around the bottom edge of the nail, where it joins your finger) back towards the finger. Don't push too hard, it hurts!
- **Important:** never cut the cuticle.

5 The finishing touch (A hand massage will earn you the big tips!)

- With a generous squeeze of hand lotion, firmly rub it into the hand, making sure you go between the fingers and along them.
- Apply pressure to the palm of the hand, the flashy pad at the base of the thumb and the webbing between thumb and forefinger. This should all be in flowing movements.
- Remember, you've just spent a while making the hand look perfect—don't crush it!

Getting colourful

Here's how to apply nail polish:

1 The foundation

You'll need a base coat or nail hardener.
Start at the base of the nail and apply even strokes out to the edge.
This layer will ensure a smooth finish after you apply the colour.

2 Paint!

Once the base coat is dry (10 minutes or so) you can apply the colour.
It's the same process as the foundation: start at the base and sweep out to the edge.
Don't paint the finger tip! You can give a second coat once the first is completely dry.

3 Top It off

Apply a clear layer of varnish to protect your masterwork and give the nails a professional shine.

OUTDOORS

Pearl diver

Traditional pearl diving (*ama*) is 2,000 years old. Originally, the divers were mostly women, who dove about 30m (100ft) without any breathing apparatus. Today *ama* has been supplanted by cultured pearl farms. Some *ama* divers remain, but they work mostly in the tourist industry.

Ama: the old way

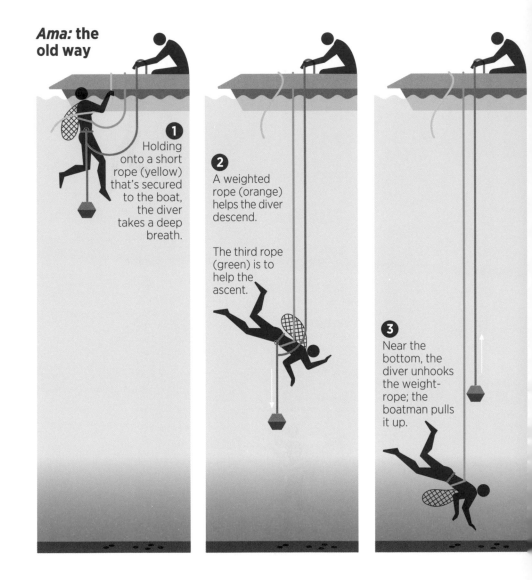

1 Holding onto a short rope (yellow) that's secured to the boat, the diver takes a deep breath.

2 A weighted rope (orange) helps the diver descend.

The third rope (green) is to help the ascent.

3 Near the bottom, the diver unhooks the weight-rope; the boatman pulls it up.

Before the advent of pearl farms, more than
a ton of pearl oysters had to be collected by hand
to find three or four quality pearls.

4
The diver collects oysters and puts them in the basket.

5
When the diver needs to come up for air, she tugs on the rope, and the boatman pulls her up.

6
Back at the surface, the diver takes a 5-minute break, then dives again.

Typically divers will descend 10 times in a session, and stay down for an average of 3.5 minutes.

 Navigator

To navigate, you've got to know where you are going.
But oops, you can't find your compass. (Not a good start
to your navigation career!)

Fear not! Here are four ways to find what direction you are facing, without a compass.

1 during the day ... **2**

Sunrise

- First thing in the morning, the sun is east-ish. But it varies through the year, sometimes actually rising in the east, but at others rising more towards the northeast or southeast.

Approximate sunrise directions

Stick and shadow

- The shortest shadow cast by a stick is a perfect north-south line anywhere in the world, and this happens at midday.

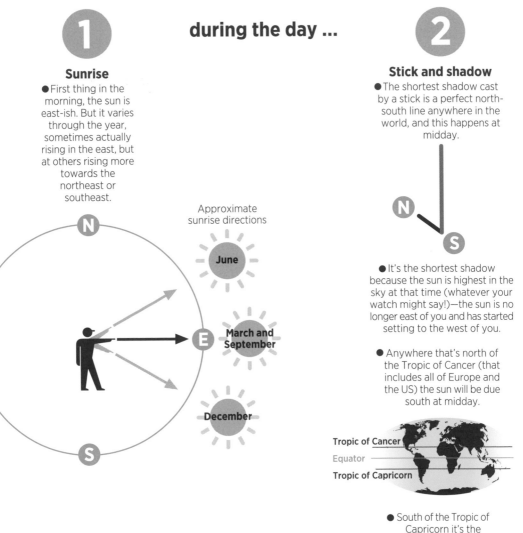

- It's the shortest shadow because the sun is highest in the sky at that time (whatever your watch might say!)—the sun is no longer east of you and has started setting to the west of you.

- Anywhere that's north of the Tropic of Cancer (that includes all of Europe and the US) the sun will be due south at midday.

Tropic of Cancer
Equator
Tropic of Capricorn

- South of the Tropic of Capricorn it's the other way round.

3

or at night

4

Moon

- If the moon is in a crescent phase, imagine a line running from its top tip past the bottom tip and all the way down to earth's horizon.

- If you're in the Northern Hemisphere, the point where the line touches the ground is due south from where you are.

- In the Southern Hemisphere, where the line touches the ground is due north.

Stars

- Place a straight stick on a tall rock or tree limb. Make sure it's steady.

- Stand or lie in a position you can copy later.

Tip: mark the position of your fist on the rock so you always go back to exactly the same position.

- Using the stick as a sight, line it up with a bright star that you can recognize later.

- Come back in half an hour and notice which direction the star has moved—

if it's moved to the right, you are facing south.

moved left, = facing north

moved up, = facing east

moved down, = facing west

The star may have moved up and right or down and right slightly, so you will have to estimate direction, such as southeast or southwest.

Gondolier

There are 425 licensed gondoliers in Venice. All men. Except for one: the first woman got her license in 2010.

Seven things you need to know

1 You don't have to sing. But tourists will always ask for O Sole Mio...

So here's what you say: "There are two kinds of people, singers and lovers. (Slight pause) I don't sing."

2 Be ready for a real workout. You need good upper body strength.

3 This weird thing is the forcola. You rest the oar—it's not a pole—in various positions on it, depending where you are steering the gondola.

4 Steering is vital (no bumping the sides of the narrow canals). How to back up is equally important.

5 Speaking of backing up, you should have a mental map of the many canals, and which are the prettiest.

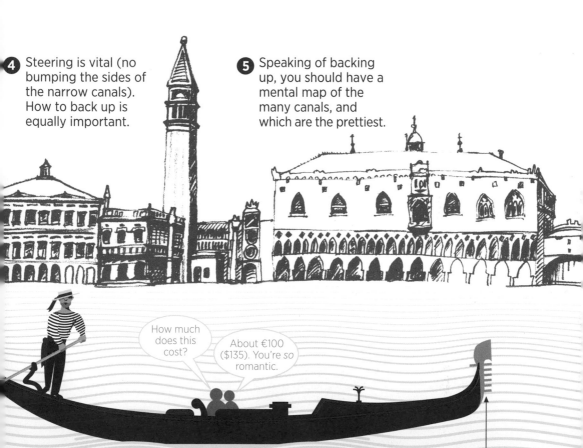

How much does this cost?

About €100 ($135). You're *so* romantic.

6 The flat-bottomed boat is very tippy, and its hull is deliberately built to veer to the right. To counter this, the gondolier must keep the oar in the water on the right side to push against the gondola's directional pull.

7 You don't really *need* to know this, but that heavy metal shape on the prow is full of meaning. (It's also a counterbalance to the gondolier at the other end.)

The whole thing is called the ferro, and it's a virtual Venice geography lesson: for instance, the six prongs stand for the six government divisions of the city.

71

Dog walker

You might think that taking dogs for a walk would be fun, or be good exercise, or that it might turn into a job, but first you must really love dogs.

I mean, do you have a car sticker like this?

Starting out

 Ask friends if you can walk their dogs so you can get a little practice. A little later, if it goes well, get references from the owners.

 Some schools offer **dog-walking certification** (and some cities require it). Find out what's available in your area.

 Know your city or local area. Check out what dog-walking laws apply to you. For instance, what to do about dog bites, and the importance of keeping rabies vaccinations up to date.

How many dogs can I take at one time?

 If this is to be your business, think about how many dogs you can take on a walk at one time. **Start with just one or two.** When you have more confidence, perhaps you can go up to five.

 You must learn **which breeds get on with others,** let alone the personalities (dogalties?) of the animals you group together.

The way to walk

 Remember, **dogs are pack animals,** but you lead the pack! The dogs should walk beside or slightly behind you, but never in front. It's very important to show them that **you are the leader.**

 Do not let dogs off the leash, except in special dog-run areas. And even then always keeps your dogs in your view.

 In cold weather, wear warm clothes—but don't worry too much about the dogs, they naturally regulate their temperature.

 Carry some **water** with you and a collapsible drinking bowl, especially on hot days. You never know what keep you outside longer than you had planned. Of course, take plastic **poop bags** (more than one), and use them!

Woof, woofetty, woof.*

Translation:
"That looks like fun. Can I join the pack?"

Mountain guide

First thing: climbing is **dangerous** and takes time to master. Begin with easy climbs and progress to harder climbs as you gain experience.

❶ Get fit!

It's a very demanding occupation. If you think you can just go climbing after sitting at a desk all day, I'm afraid you are wrong. Train for fitness and strength in ways that benefit you best.

Try these fitness regimens:

running and jogging, including endurance running

walking and hiking, with the hiking getting increasingly arduous

weightlifting, or walking/running with weights in a backpack or in your hands

practising climbing on a local wall, or taking ice-climbing lessons

skiing or snow-boarding (especially if you intend to descend that way: extreme, but possible on some mountains!)

anything that helps you **improve strength and endurance—** essentials for complete mountain-climbing fitness

❷ Be a safe climber: some tips

Plan carefully: you must have information about the length and difficulty of your climb to be sure of a safe experience on the mountain. **Tell others where you are going.**

Be realistic about your level of fitness, and choose suitable hikes or climbs. Start early in the morning and build extra time into your plan, to make sure you are back before it gets dark.

Make sure you **take plenty of fluids:** water, tea or natural juices are the best. Take foods rich in nutrients, such as wholemeal bread, dried fruits and nuts

Before you go, study the **latest weather forecast.** Then keep watching conditions while you are climbing.

Always follow the path and stay on marked trails. Consult your map: in case of doubt turn back in good time.

Here we go!

❸ Take the right gear

You'll need this **essential equipment** → to keep your clients (and yourself!) safe.

Belay device
Prevents climbers from falling

Grappling hook
This allows you to create a grip on the rock

Carabiners
Different types and shapes have many uses (e.g., clip yourself or your gear to the rock face).

Helmet
Falling rock or chunks of ice can really spoil your day!

Climbing rope
Attached to the rock wall as the lead climber goes up.

Backpack
Food and drink! Plus first aid kit. (Perhaps even a tent.)

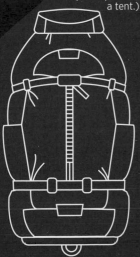

Harness
Worn snugly on the hips, it attaches climber to rope—it's a safety net. It's also used to carry gear.

Crampons
For extra grippage.

Oceanographer

Since 71% of the planet is covered with water, it seems like a good idea to study the ocean—the five named oceans are all connected, so we are in effect awash in a one big sea. Yet we know more about outer space than we do about the waters around us.

dry

wet

Oceanographers study currents, marine life, the sea floor, stuff like that. Here are five big questions for them:

house

❶ Why is the sea so angry?

Global climate change seems to be whipping up bigger and bigger storms. The 2004 Indian Ocean tsunami produced waves on land that reached 30m (100ft) high. 230,000 people died.

❷ You're going to drink that?

With drinking water in short supply in many parts of the world, scientists are trying to find economic ways to desalinate the oceans. Today, the countries most active in getting the salt out of sea water are in the Middle East and North Africa, but it's expensive, and the cost has kept desalination from becoming widespread.

This is lifesize. Pretty small!

❸ Anything living down here?

No human could withstand the pressure. Sorry, no mermaids. You couldn't see them anyway: there's no light after you've gone down more than 150m (500 ft). However, certain species of angler fish can survive; and with their bioluminescent* appendages they hunt for food in the Mariana Trench, in the Western Pacific, which is around 10km (6.2 miles) deep.

* Only one other animal with this facility: fireflies!

Arctic
14.1 million sq km (5.4 million sq miles)

Atlantic
76.8 million sq km
(29.7 million sq miles)

Indian
68.6 million sq km
(26.5 million sq miles)

Pacific
155.6 million sq km
(60 million sq miles)

Pacific (again!)

Southern (Antarctic)
20.3 million sq km
(7.8 million sq miles)

⑥ What's all that garbage?

We throw a lot of stuff away. And **a lot of it** ends up in these two "garbage patches" in the Pacific.

Currents gather it into swirling masses of (mostly) plastic. It's only partly visible from the surface, but it's deadly to marine animals, which choke to death on our discarded shopping bags and non-biodegradable cups and water (!) bottles.

⑤ How deep is the ocean?

**Average:
4.3km
(2.6 miles)**

The Challenger Deep, in the Mariana Trench, near Guam, is the **deepest: 11km (6.9 miles)**

If the highest mountain on land sat on the bottom of the ocean here, its summit would not reach the ocean's surface. (Mount Everest is 8.8km (5.5 miles) high.)

Bird watcher

What's weird about this picture? The ears, right? But that's the point: your ears are almost as important as your eyes when you are birdwatching.

1 Learn bird sounds

Lots of apps let you hear different songs. Outdoors, these songs are your first clues to what birds might be in the area that you are watching.

2 Match illustrations to sounds

A good guidebook's pictures should also indicate the typical heights or locations that specific birds perch.

Hello. Anyone in there?

Mallard

③ Now you know what you are looking for
Focus on where the sounds come from.
Up high? Eye level? On the ground?

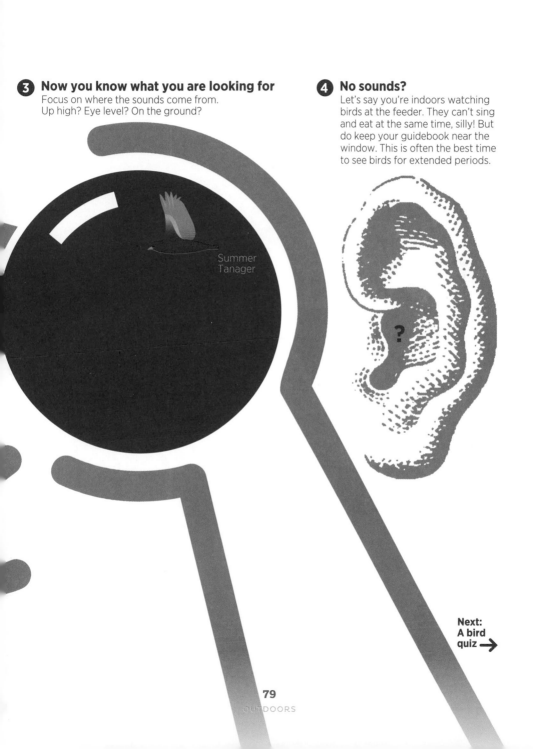

Summer
Tanager

④ No sounds?
Let's say you're indoors watching birds at the feeder. They can't sing and eat at the same time, silly! But do keep your guidebook near the window. This is often the best time to see birds for extended periods.

**Next:
A bird
quiz →**

Of course, the birds you'll see depends on where you go.

There are no parakeets in Paris, no penguins in Portugal, and no toucans in Tokyo*, but dedicated birdwatchers would go pretty much anywhere if they thought the trip would add another bird to their personal checklist of sightings.

Can you name these very different birds?

As a newly dedicated birdwatcher you'll have to do some travelling to see them for yourselves.

*As far as we know ... But alright readers, tell us we're wrong, (Zoos and pets don't count.)

1. Northern Cardinal
2. California Condor
3. Scarlet Macaw
4. Toco Toucan
5. Yellow-tailed Black Cockatoo
6. Blue Tit
7. Secretary Bird
8. Red-throated Parrot Finch
9. Mandarin Duck

Caber tosser

Scotland's Highland games are held in many locations throughout the year to celebrate Scottish and Celtic culture. One of the "heavy" competitions, **tossing the caber,** has come to symbolise the whole gathering.

The caber (from the Gaelic word for a wooden beam) is typically made from a larch tree. It's 5.94m (19.5ft) long and weighs 79kg (175lb).

The sport is thought to have been developed from tossing logs across ditches to make a bridge.

1 The competitor balances the caber on his shoulder (with the help of friends) and starts a short run forward, keeping the pole balanced in front of him. (Not as easy as you might think given its weight and length.)

2 He stops and lets the caber swing forward.

3 Lifting the caber as high as he can, he thrusts it up into the air.

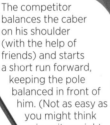

They toss cabers in other countries too!
Worldwide Highland games

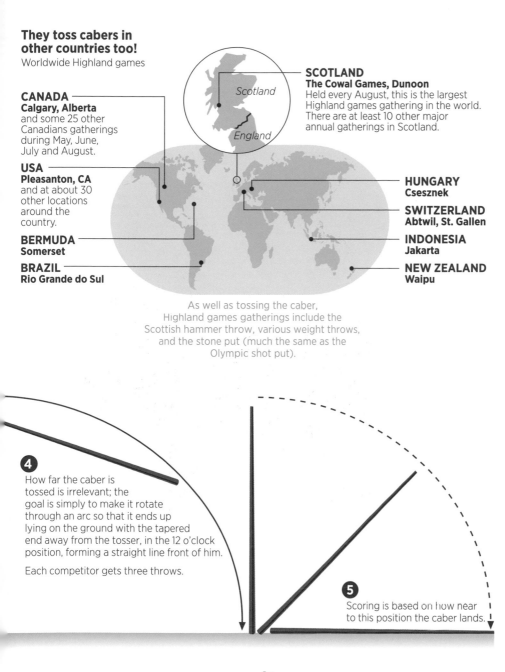

CANADA
Calgary, Alberta
and some 25 other Canadians gatherings during May, June, July and August.

USA
Pleasanton, CA
and at about 30 other locations around the country.

BERMUDA
Somerset

BRAZIL
Rio Grande do Sul

SCOTLAND
The Cowal Games, Dunoon
Held every August, this is the largest Highland games gathering in the world. There are at least 10 other major annual gatherings in Scotland.

HUNGARY
Csesznek

SWITZERLAND
Abtwil, St. Gallen

INDONESIA
Jakarta

NEW ZEALAND
Waipu

Scotland

England

As well as tossing the caber, Highland games gatherings include the Scottish hammer throw, various weight throws, and the stone put (much the same as the Olympic shot put).

4
How far the caber is tossed is irrelevant; the goal is simply to make it rotate through an arc so that it ends up lying on the ground with the tapered end away from the tosser, in the 12 o'clock position, forming a straight line front of him.

Each competitor gets three throws.

5
Scoring is based on how near to this position the caber lands.

Inuit hunter

Living in the freezing far north of Canada, where there isn't a lot of vegetation, means that the native Inuit have learned how to be year-round animal hunters. And they use everything from their catches: meat, pelts, horns, antlers, blubber, *everything*.

Want to go along?
Here's what you'd be looking for **on land:**

But first, you must dress for harsh weather. Look at this traditional Inuit clothing—they know how to keep (fashionably!) warm.

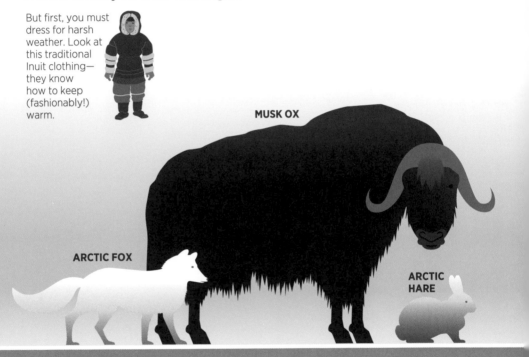

MUSK OX

ARCTIC FOX

ARCTIC HARE

The pelts of Arctic foxes used to be an important trading commodity (often for rifles), but today they are mostly used for **meat and clothing.** Inuit women wear the tails as scarves or hood trims and the tail tendons can be used as sewing thread.

Musk oxen are hunted for their **warm woolly coats, horns, and meat.** Since fuel for cooking is scarce, the Inuit often eat meat raw. Of course it's easy to preserve what's left by freezing it.

Yes, Arctic hares are cute. But the **meat** is tasty. (Sorry, vegetarians—it's just too cold for most plants to survive; the hares themselves have to claw through crusty snow for roots of dwarf willow, their main food source.)

Old tools ...

and new

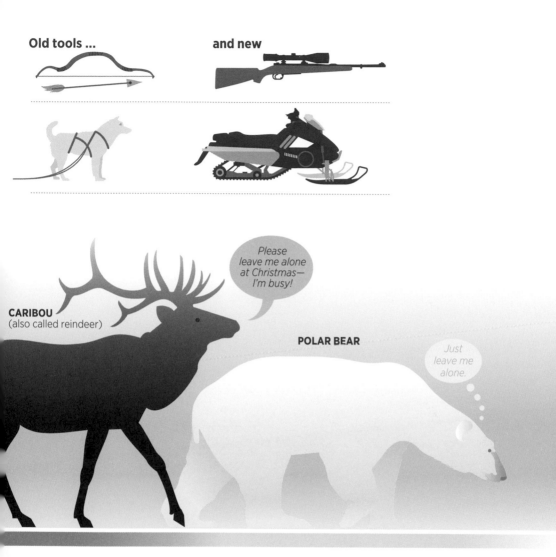

CARIBOU
(also called reindeer)

Please leave me alone at Christmas—I'm busy!

POLAR BEAR

Just leave me alone.

Finding caribou is difficult because they have excellent hearing and sense of smell. They are hunted for **meat**, and the tips of their antlers make sharp **harpoon tips.**

Traditionally, Polar bear fur was made into **warm clothing,** but overhunting has depleted bear populations, and today, native peoples are the only ones legally allowed to hunt them—and there's a strict quota. Norway bans hunting completely.

Next: hunting on ice and in water →

Thought hunting on land was cold? Now get wet!

If you join the Inuit, here's what you'll be hunting **on ice and in water:**

WALRUS

Seals are hunted in **winter.** Because of thick ice, they have to come up to the surface to use breathing holes. Hunters wait and harpoon them.

HOODED SEAL

BELUGA WHALE

The walrus is important for its **meat, fat, skin, tusks and bone.** The meat is especially valuable since it does not spoil quickly, making it good for long hunting trips.

Beluga whales are valued for their **skins, meat and blubber.** Their skin is the only whale skin that's thick enough to be used as leather. As with Polar bears, Inuit hunting is strictly controlled.

Like belugas, seals are hunted for their **skins, meat and blubber.** Seal meat is an essential element of the Inuit diet, and Inuit sometimes drink seal blood.

In **summer,** Inuits go out in kayaks that were originally made from skins (often seal skins) stretched over a wood or whalebone frame.

ARCTIC CHAR

NARWHAL

What exactly is blubber?

It's a thick layer of tissue under the skin—insulation for whales and seals— that is important to Inuit diet. (It contains vitamins E and D, and omega-3 fatty acids.) Blubber can also be rendered into oil and used to make soap, candlewax and fuel for lamps.

Narwhals are hunted for their splendid **tusks, oil, skin and meat** (but the meat is generally fed to dogs).

The **flesh** of Arctic char ranges from deep red to pink and tastes a bit like salmon. Arctic char is one of very few freshwater fishes found in the far North. The Inuit catch them by dangling a fake fish from a short line, and then harpoon them when they approach the bait.

Smokejumper

The Twin Otter turbine engine DC-3 is one of a small group of planes used for jumpers.

Some brave people jump out of planes into a blazing fire zone. *On purpose.* They are specialist firefighters whose job is to contain wildfires. Clearly, it's not a job for the faint-hearted.

You have to be pretty fit.
In California* these are the
minimum physical requirements:

- do 7 pull-ups
- do 25 push-ups
- do 45 sit-ups
- run 4.8km (1.5 miles) in 11 minutes
- carry 50kg (110lb) pack 3 miles in 90 minutes
  (You'll be carrying your kit for days, perhaps weeks, in the wild.)

and you must:
- be at least 18 years old
- be a minimum of 1.5m (5ft) and a maximum of 2m (6ft 5in) tall
- weigh at least 55kg (120lbs) but no more than 90kg (200lbs)

*Smokejumpers operate mostly in western US, and Russia.

Previous parachuting experience is neither required nor advantageous when you apply for a job. But you do need guts.

Before you jump, there's a tough training period: you'll be taught how to land in rough, forested terrain. (Part of the equipment you carry is a rope in case you land in a tree.)

Smokejumper skills

- Tree climbing
- Tree felling with cross-cut saws and chainsaws
- Digging fire trenches up to 1m (3ft) wide
- Navigation with map and compass
- Fire evaluation— its direction and speed; weather considerations
- First aid

wire mesh facemask

high collar for tree landings

padded Kevlar jacket and pants

reserve parachute

personal gearbag

rope for tree landings in leg pockets

Mechanical saws, shovels, Pulaskis (half-pick, half axe) and McLeods (part rake, part shovel) are dropped into the firezone separately.

Jockey

You really do have to love horses to be a jockey—you'll be spending a lot of time with them. A lot!

1 The number one requirement if you want to be a jockey is **commitment.** You'll be getting up early seven days a week. There'll be lots of ground work, mucking out the stables, learning about horse care and watching the more experienced apprentices.

2 **Height** is important; the smaller you are, the easier it will be for you to make the necessary weight. The average jockey is around 1.5m (5ft 2in), but some are taller. Lester Piggot was nearly 1.7m (5ft 8in), but he was very skinny!

3 **Weight is much more important than height.** You should weigh no more than 50kg (110 lb).

4 Your **diet** will be pretty harsh. To keep the weight down you have to watch the calorie intake. Often jockeys have nothing more than a few cups of tea and some toast during the day.

5 You must be **16 years old** or more to get into an apprentice school or work directly with a trainer. In Spain you can ride in races as an amateur at 14.

6 It barely needs to be said that you must be **fit!** You'll be riding every day. At first you'll be just exercising the horses. But if you become a successful jockey you, could be riding 12 races in one day, flying from one race meeting to another!

7 **Are you fearless?** It's a dangerous sport.

 **The best jockeys know the strengths of each horse** they ride, and how to position them during the first part of the race, so that they can come through with a strong finish.

It's all about the hands. Instead of trying to out-muscle a horse, good jockeys control and guide their mounts with "good hands"—calm, quiet, feeling the reins. The horse can tell!

Pit crew member

HOW TO BE A ...

NASCAR (National Association of Stock Car Racing), was once a solely American motorsport. Now it's gaining followers in Europe. There are many pit stops during the long races. The next time your rental car gets a puncture, here's how quickly a pro pit crew would fix it.

6 crew members

jump over the retaining wall when their car has passed the back line of the pit before their own.

If any of the crew jumps early, the team is penalised 15 seconds.

After the leader begins lapping slower cars, and the race organizers give the OK, a 7th crew member is allowed onto the pit area to clean the windscreen and supply the driver with water.

Tyre carrier

at back hands new wheel to the changer.

Gas man

inserts a 42L (11gals) fuel can into the car's tank.

Jackman

raises right side of car, so wheels can be changed.

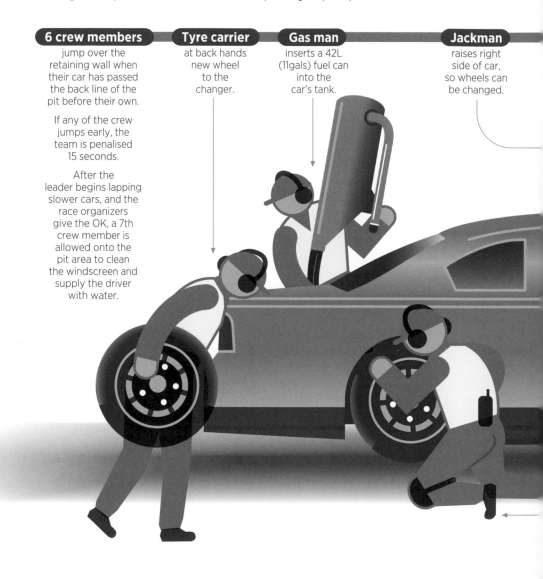

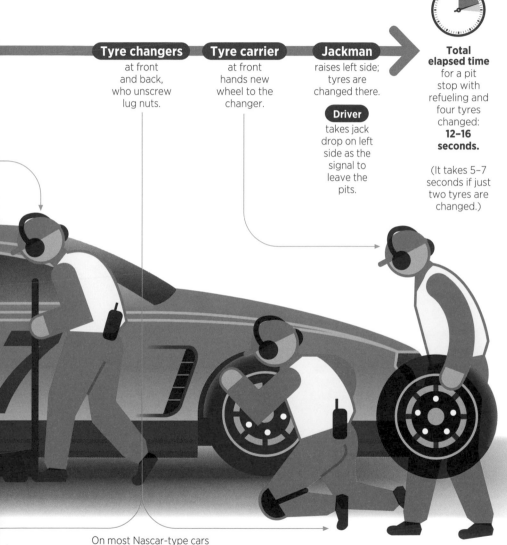

Tyre changers
at front
and back,
who unscrew
lug nuts.

Tyre carrier
at front
hands new
wheel to the
changer.

Jackman
raises left side;
tyres are
changed there.

Driver
takes jack
drop on left
side as the
signal to
leave the
pits.

**Total
elapsed time**
for a pit
stop with
refueling and
four tyres
changed:
**12–16
seconds.**

(It takes 5–7
seconds if just
two tyres are
changed.)

On most Nascar-type cars
there are five nuts on the wheels.
(On Formula One cars, there's just one.)

Climatologist

Most scientists agree that our changing climate is man-made.

Unlike TV weather forecasters, climatologists are not trying to predict day-to-day weather. Their job has evolved into issuing warnings about the long-term effects. **Here are signs of climate change that climatologists are urging us all to heed.**

1 Perhaps the most important result of increasing temperatures is the rising ocean

- **Polar icecaps** have melted faster in the last 20 years than in the whole of the last 10,000. Scientists now say that this melt is unstoppable, and that sea levels could rise by 3 feet or more by 2100.

- **Coastal cities** in the US, home to more than 3.7 million, will be inundated. The **Maldive Islands** in the the Indian Ocean will completely disappear.

- Many animal species are threatened, among them **Adélie penguins** on Antarctica, and **Polar bears** in the Arctic. They face extinction because their habitats are disappearing.

2 More rain
(much more)

- Climatologists calculate that just in the US **global warming has put an extra 3.7 trillion litres (1 trillion gallons) of water into the air.**

- **This has to fall** as rain or snow, and that's why rain- and snow-storms will be more frequent and of greater ferocity.

3 Conflicts

- It's said that the next major war will be fought over **water rights, food and land.**

- Some experts believe that the conflict in **Darfur, Sudan,** was partially caused by a warmer climate—especially because it reduced natural resources, and that led to refugees fighting settled farmers food sources.

4 Hunger

- Moderate warming and increased carbon (CO_2) in the atmosphere help plants grow faster, but if the warming trend continues at the current rate, **floods and drought will reduce crop yields.**

- **Fisheries** are adversely affected by warming water temperatures; this makes the water hospitable to invasive species and alters lifecycle timing.

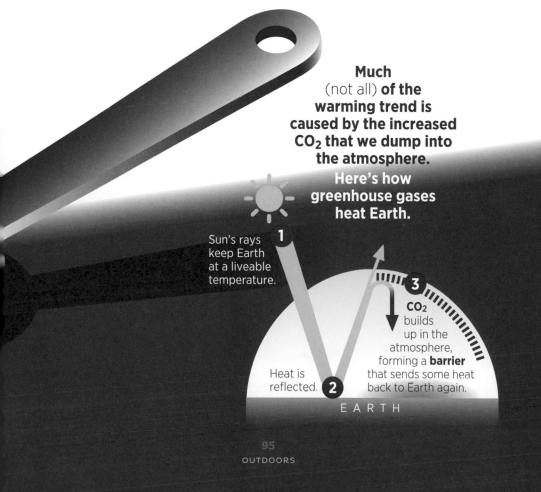

Much (not all) **of the warming trend is caused by the increased CO_2 that we dump into the atmosphere.**

Here's how greenhouse gases heat Earth.

Sun's rays keep Earth at a liveable temperature. **1**

Heat is reflected. **2**

3 CO_2 builds up in the atmosphere, forming a **barrier** that sends some heat back to Earth again.

EARTH

Speedskater

Like many sports, speedskating has taken advantage of technology. So if you want to compete in world-class events, get yourself a pair of **clap skates.**

(You do know how to skate, right? That's kind of important too.)

Clap skates were invented by the Dutch around 2000. Not coincidentally, athletes from the Netherlands hold many world records in the sport.

1 The **clap skate** allows the edge of a blade to remain in full contact with the ice for an extra moment, even though the foot is beginning to lift off.

2 The brief added contact with the ice means that a skater can exert more force on the blade, which in turn generates **more speed.**

Under the ice, pipes containing **liquid refrigerant** are embedded in a perfectly flat cement floor.

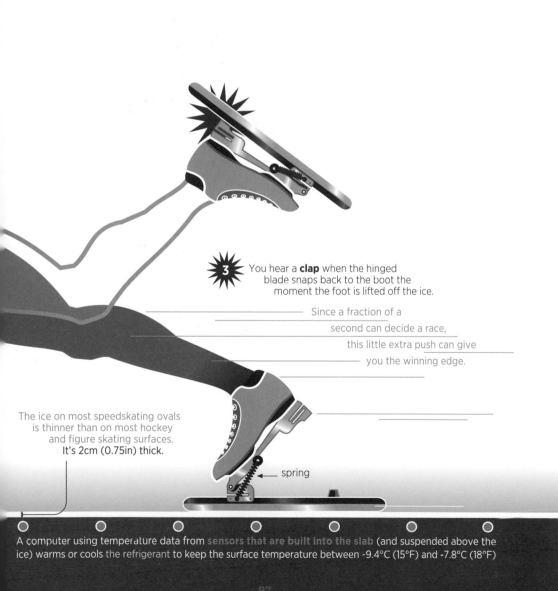

3 You hear a **clap** when the hinged blade snaps back to the boot the moment the foot is lifted off the ice.

Since a fraction of a second can decide a race, this little extra push can give you the winning edge.

The ice on most speedskating ovals is thinner than on most hockey and figure skating surfaces. It's 2cm (0.75in) thick.

spring

A computer using temperature data from sensors that are built into the slab (and suspended above the ice) warms or cools the refrigerant to keep the surface temperature between -9.4°C (15°F) and -7.8°C (18°F)

HOW TO BE A ...

Hiking guide

Sure, you need a backpack, maps and a compass, a first aid kit for your clients, and food and water for yourself. But if you can **carry less** you'll keep going much longer.

See what happens when you take a load off your back.

2.5kg (5lb)

4.5kg (10lb)

11.5kg (25lb)

Uneven ground plays havoc with your legs, adding **pressure on your knees.** When you lighten the load you carry; your knees will thank you!

98

INSTANT EXPERT

Reducing the load

Shop around on the web for lightweight gear
(representative weights shown here).

- Depending on its capacity, the **backpack** itself should be light. You can find
packs with enough room for a three-day hike starting around 0.5kg (15oz).

Some of the other items you'll be taking:
- sleeping bag 0.5kg (16oz) ● sleeping pad 0.25kg (9oz) ● shelter (tent) 0.18kg (6.3oz).
- rain gear 0.3kg (10oz) ● stove 0.06kg (2oz) ● fuel 0.2kg (7oz)

Take food out of the packaging it comes in,
and put it into plastic bags.

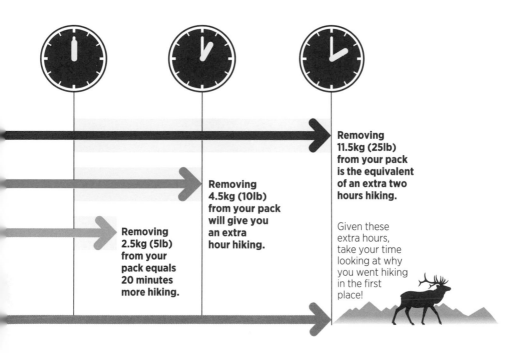

Removing
2.5kg (5lb)
from your
pack equals
20 minutes
more hiking.

Removing
4.5kg (10lb)
from your pack
will give you
an extra
hour hiking.

Removing
11.5kg (25lb)
from your pack
is the equivalent
of an extra two
hours hiking.

Given these
extra hours,
take your time
looking at why
you went hiking
in the first
place!

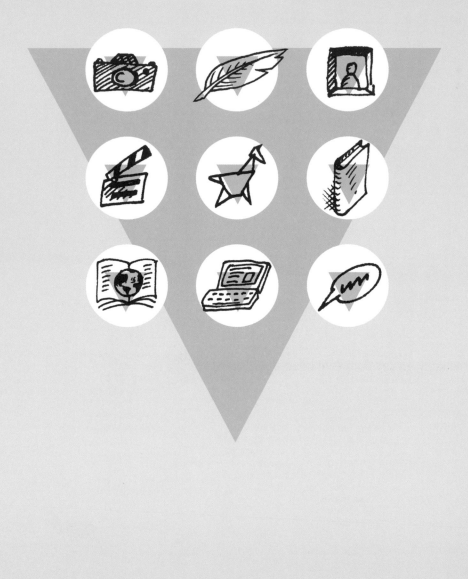

ARTS AND CULTURE

 Photographer

There's a story about a young man who told Andy Warhol that he wanted to be a photographer. Warhol said that if he told people he was a photographer, then he would be one.

And most of us have cameras. (A report in 2014 found that there were 6 billion mobile phone subscriptions—that's in a world population of just a bit more than 7 billion people.)

Of course, there are better cameras than the ones we have in our mobile phones, but photography is about much more than the equipment; it's about **looking.**

13 tips for better pix (and one gentle warning)

Take lots of pictures, then throw most of them away. But learn from the bad ones: don't take pictures like that again!

Ignore tip number one! **Patience, patience, patience.** In many cases, you just have to wait until it's the right moment.

Here he is!

3 **Turn the camera on its side.**
A regular camera is usually configured to take horizontal pictures when you hold it; most mobile phone cameras are set up more naturally to take vertical ones. Some subjects look much better as vertical pictures, and others look better as horizontals.

OK

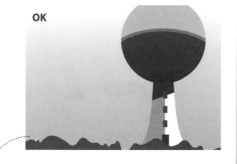

better

3a **Don't forget black and white. Stylish.**

4 **Use simple backgrounds.** When taking pictures of people, avoid distractions behind the subject.

dreadful

better

Next: more tips →

The tips keep coming

5 It sounds wrong, but it's best to **use flash outdoors** on bright sunny days. The sun can make harsh shadows, especially on faces.

6 **Ask permission** before taking pictures of performers (or anyone you don't know). Offer to send them prints, or digital files.

7 When framing a picture, move the main subject **away from the centre.**

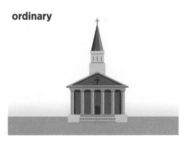

ordinary

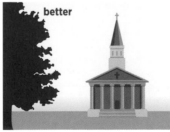

better

8 Your flash will illuminate only a limited distance from the camera. So when using **flash indoors,** anything that's more than about five steps away will be dark.

who *is* that?

aha!

10 Great times to take pictures are during the **golden hours.** These are just after sunrise or just before sunset, when daylight is redder and softer (and colours are brighter) than when the sun is higher in the sky.

Also, you might try taking pictures during the so-called **blue hours**—twilight—neither full daylight nor complete darkness.

11 When people are posing for you, tell a quick **joke** instead of getting them to say cheese. Better a laugh than a forced smile.

Heard the one about ... ?

12 **Archive** your pictures by date as well as event. You'd be surprised at how soon you will forget the date, even the year, of that birthday party, or exactly when it was that you visited the Tower of Pisa on the Italy vacation.

13 **Put the camera away and enjoy the view.** At least enjoy the view before you start snapping away—after all, you've come a long way to visit a beautiful village or a spectacular destination; how do you know what to shoot if you don't look first?

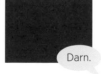

! Take the lens cap off!

Darn.

Next: Breaking the rules →

Now forget the rules!

Your best shots might just result from *not* following photography's golden rules.

Motion
● If it's blurry, don't wurry! The music moves and you're a bit tipsy It doesn't matter: you've captured the spirit. Don't throw your 'mistakes' away.

Guilty pleasure
● Remember that delicious hot dog with the perfect mustard squiggle after a visit to the museum?

Your point of view
● Don't just shoot from a standing position. Crouch. Lie down. Climb up.

A hole in → the middle
● It may seem like bad composition but there's nothing wrong with nothing in the centre of your picture.

← Back lighting
● Shoot *into* the sun for terrific silhouette pictures. (Not for faces, though!)

Buy the classic cliché
● At touristy hotspots, get postcards. (Send them to loved ones, with real handwriting and stamps). This leaves you more time to see the unexpected.

Next: → seeking colour

Not what's right in front of you
● Look up!

No posing
● Snap a picture when they don't know you are looking. Much more life.

Stolen moment
● Be ready when she suddenly turns.

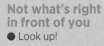

Get close
● Get *really* close!

Colour, just colour!

Sometimes it's worth taking a little time to notice a beautiful shade of green, or blue, or red, or...

Magenta and orange poison; pink and green; autumn's reds and ochres; yellow in the middle; running red; blue eye.

Apple green; immaculate shiny green;
fractal cauliflower green; seeing blue.
Winter's white: a colour, too.

Poet

"You're a poet and you don't know it."

Of course, poems don't have to rhyme—'tho* many do. (There's even an academic movement that proves Shakespeare's sonnets rhyme.)**

So let's write a rhyming poem. Together.

1 **Wander into a field of poppies and stick your head in the clouds.**

*A poemy word, that.

**Sonnets are supposed to rhyme, but 96 of Shakespeare's 154 sonnets don't—until you pronounce the words the way people spoke them in Shakespeare's time.

❷ Fill in the blanks with your poetry.

You can make every line rhyme or add other lines in between that don't. Here are some line-ending rhyme hints. Move them around to suit your poem.

Just to get you going: *The poppies are blooming, it must be* [J F M / A M / J A S / O N D] (J)

And I will spend the 🕐

Now you take over: ....

....

....

....

....

....

❸ For words that don't end in "oon," get a rhyming dictionary.

(There are several online dictionaries, too.) Some words are difficult to rhyme. Orange, for instance.

Surely there's more to poetry than this?

Well, I *could* tell you about iambic pentameter, dactylic hexameter, enjambment, caesura, anapest, quatrain, spondee ...

Oh, that's OK, I'll stick with rhyme.

 # Art critic

Long ago, art was simple. A rich patron—often the church—told artists what to paint. People understood the result. They got the point. They could *see* the point.

Today however, we need specialists to tell us what we are looking at.
Let's consider four art pieces from the past. Art critics discuss the kind of comments like these that you often hear in galleries:

It gives me a headache! Is that the point?

This costs five million dollars?

The art movement called Op Art was popular in the 1960s. **Bridget Riley** and other artists dazzled the eye with precisely drawn lines and shapes, creating a visual flicker from still images.

Are these actual paintings?

Not exactly— they're drawn to look like examples of the artists' work.

In the 2000s, **Damien Hirst** (or one of his many assistants) poured paint onto huge turntables and flipped a switch to produce very expensive splatter art.

Why is this "art" at all? It's a balloon animal.

Well, yes,
Jeff Koons
is inspired by cheap, kitschy trinkets. Like Hirst, Koons employs assistants who manufacture his immaculately made sculptures, which are shined up to a glassy perfection.

My kid could have done this!

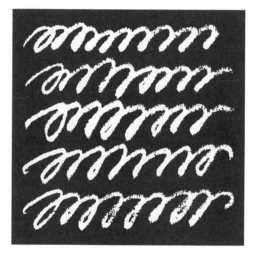

Cy Twombly's
apparently haphazard and childish scribble-paintings do appear to be dashed off. But he's considered an influential figure in modern art.

Next: Opinions are subjective ➔

Art criticism is very subjective,

and well-known critics have plenty of critics of their own!
But it's their job to make people think about the meaning of art,
and sometimes their opinions cause trouble.

Basics

Ways a critic might
start thinking about
a picture or sculpture.

 Describe the piece.
What colours, shapes,
textures are used?
Is it abstract or
pictorial? What
materials are used?
(Oil, water-colour,
collage, mixed
media, etc.)

2 **Explain the
artistic influence.**
Almost all art can
be identified as
belonging to an
existing school,
or genre, or art
movement.

3 **Provide a context.**
What else was going
on in the art world
when this piece was
produced? Does it
break new ground?

4 **Aesthetics versus
shock value.**
Is the piece beautiful,
or is it just meant to
provoke a specific
reaction?

Art history

It's not the same as art criticism, but a critic must know
enough of the history to be able to explain art to others.
and must study hundreds of art movements.

Who's the person in this famous picture?

Scarlett Johansson
played her in *The Girl
with the Pearl Earring*
about Vermeer's 1665
painting, but the
painter's actual sitter is
unknown, on purpose—
it's an example of
"genre" painting,
representing a class of
person not an
individual.

Why is the sky red in Edvard Munch's famous *Scream* (1893)?

One theory is that after
the 1883 Krakatoa
eruption the skies half
a world away were
tinted with bright
colours. Munch saw this
and used it a decade
later to heighten the
expressionist mood of
his picture.

Movements galore (a selection, starting in the 19th century)

art nouveau • art deco • impressionism • post-impressionism • pointillism
cubism • fauvism • symbolism • futurism • dada • surrealism
expressionism • minimalism • action painting • abstract expressionism
op art • pop art • photo realism • land art • performance art • graffiti

Consider these four very different
ways of painting a portrait,
spanning 400 years:

Why did Pablo Picasso fracture the surfaces of things and show them from more than one viewpoint?

With Georges Braque, Picasso invented Cubism around 1910, and he used elements of this way of painting peole and objects until his death in 1973. Cubism was a way to move images away from literal photographic reality.

Are they still called paintings when photos are printed onto the canvas?

Andy Warhol was one of a group of pop artists in the 1960s who used everyday objects, such as Campbell's soup can labels, instead of traditional art subjects. Warhol . claimed that anything could be art.

Big names in art criticism

John Ruskin (1819–1900) An artist himself, Ruskin promoted "truth to nature."

Meyer Shapiro (1904–96) supported the acquisition of early Jackson Pollock work by the Museum of Modern Art, New York, in the 1940s.

Clement Greenberg (1909–94) advocated that paintings themselves should be the subject of the paintings. Art represented itself—there was no "meaning" or pictorial reference. Greenberg also championed a "flat" style: hard-edged and geometric.

Robert Hughes (1938–2012) raised art criticism to an art in itself. His ideas in *Time* magazine and a TV series *The Shock of the New* were delivered in a learned, explanatory, funny and often ascerbic voice, but always without art jargon. Of Julian Schnabel, a painter whose work he loathed, Hughes wrote: "Schnabels's work is to painting what Stallone's is to acting: a lurching display of oily pectorals."

In an interview later, Schnabel called Hughes "a bum."

So when you become an art critic, be prepared for lots of argument!

HOW TO BE AN ...

Internet video maker

60 hours of videos are uploaded to YouTube every minute; four billion videos are viewed every day, and 70% of the traffic comes from outside the U.S., in fact the service is available in 54 languages. Here's how to make your travel video stand out from the pixel pandemonium.

① KNOW YOUR CAMERA

But first you have to buy one. It can be confusing. Do these three things:

- **Budget**
  How much do you want to spend? Is the camera on your smartphone good enough for what you want to do?

- **Try it out in the store.**
  Get the feel of it before you buy.

- **External audio jack?**
  You MUST get one that has this feature. Sound recording quality on most point-and-shoot cameras, mobile phone cameras, even expensive ($1,000+) DSLR cameras is not good enough by itself.

Familiarise yourself with your kit in a warm place so that when you're outside in the rain or snow, or under pressure from the bride's parents, **you won't press the wrong button.**

Depending on the type of camera you have, learn about **the field of view**. It's important to know what will end up in the picture and what won't.

② MIX IT UP

A cool thing about most of today's video cameras is that they are really tough, and you can put them anywhere, **so go ahead and put them anywhere!** We don't want soup made out of just peas—we want it made out of peas, potatoes and spices. **Take a bunch of angles:** at the top of the ski slope (and looking down from the ski-lift on the way up); a lone figure in the far distance; one face filling the whole frame.

This way, when you're editing, you'll have **a lot of different material to mix together.**

③ THE BEST LIGHT

Shoot in the sun, especially the "golden hour" (just after sunrise, just before sunset)—shadows are softer then.

HAVE A PLAN

Think of yourself as a storyteller. You know that a good story needs **a beginning, a middle and an end,** right? Make a plan before you start shooting. Think about how **different sequences of shots can be edited to help tell your story.**

DITCH THE GIMMICKS

Zoom should be used sparingly; **panning is banned!** (There's enough to think about when the camera is still.) Filters that distort, or add colour won't necessarily add anything to your video story. **Besides, you don't want your effort to look trendy just for the sake of it. It'll look dated pretty soon.**

6 KEEP IT SHORT

Nobody wants to see a five-minute video of you mountain biking down a trail (although a camera mounted on your head can be pretty exciting for a short time, especially if you crash). Web videos are best kept to around **60 seconds.** Watch TV commercials; you can do a lot in a minute and **it's a safe time investment for viewers.**

7 LISTEN

Built-in sound recording is seldom any good on the current crop of cameras (see the blue list, left).

Apart from an external microphone, it's easy to get sound effects—the swoosh of skis, or chirping birds— from sites like freesound.org.

And now you've made one...
HOW TO UPLOAD A VIDEO

The only thing you have to remember is that for YouTube, your file has to be less than 100 MBs, and must be in one of these formats:

.MOV	.MPEGPS
.MPEG4	.FLV
.AVI	3GPP
.WMV	WebM

The rest is easy. Go to YouTube and follow the instructions. If you are new to all this, there's lots of online help.

A FINAL TIP

Nothing here should be read as a hard and fast "rule."

Rules can cramp creativity. Break them!

Go forth and make great, short movies. (Oops, perhaps "short" *is* a rule after all! And cats? There may be enough of those cute videos online already.)

Origamist Yes, it's a word.

Origami comes from the Japanese *ori*, meaning folding, and *kami* meaning paper. Known since the 1600s, the goal is to fold a square of paper—often with a different colour on the back—into (usually) a bird or an animal. Strict origamists say no glue, no cutting.

Basic folds

Almost all origami pieces start with a combination of these simple folds.

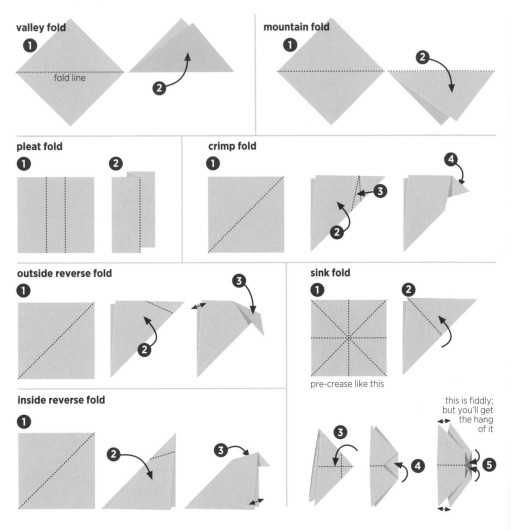

Something for a long plane ride: folding a blue and yellow crane

Use paper that's about 18cm (7in) square.

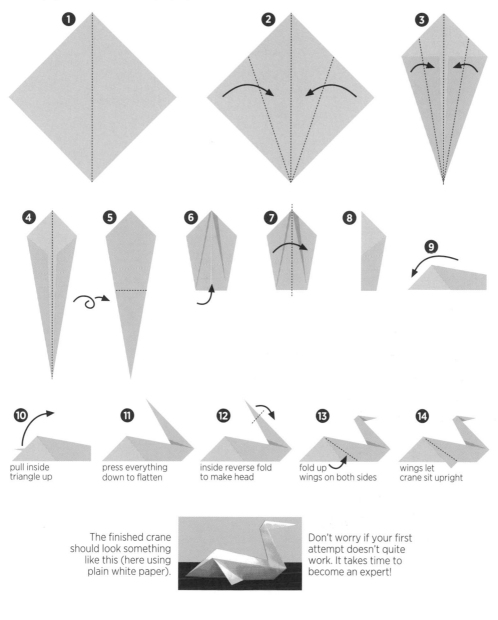

10 pull inside triangle up

11 press everything down to flatten

12 inside reverse fold to make head

13 fold up wings on both sides

14 wings let crane sit upright

The finished crane should look something like this (here using plain white paper).

Don't worry if your first attempt doesn't quite work. It takes time to become an expert!

Bookbinder

Since dead-tree books are fast becoming a thing of the past, you might think this is an odd profession to take up. But plenty of people still love books. (You bought, borrowed or stole this one, after all!)

What's more, book lovers need their books rebound. The methods used have changed only a little since the Middle Ages.

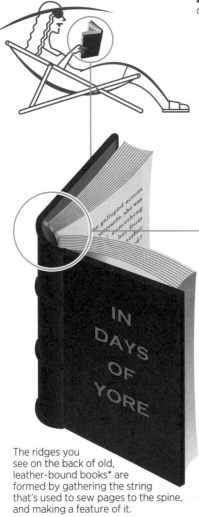

1 Traditionally, books are divided into 32-page "signatures" **A**, which are sewn to the spine lining **B**. This lining is then glued to heavy kraft paper **C**, and that in turn is glued to the boards **D**, which form the hard cover itself.

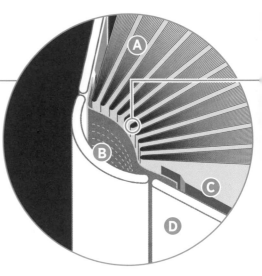

The ridges you see on the back of old, leather-bound books* are formed by gathering the string that's used to sew pages to the spine, and making a feature of it.

*Fun (or gruesome) fact: starting in the 17th century, some books were bound in human skin.
In 2014, scientists confirmed that a book in the library at Harvard University was an example of this.

2 Each signature is actually one large sheet of paper folded in half four times. (Try it with a piece of regular paper.) The folded signatures can then be sewn into the spine **E**.

3 The top, front, and bottom edges are trimmed off later, leaving 16 folded sheets, or 32 pages.

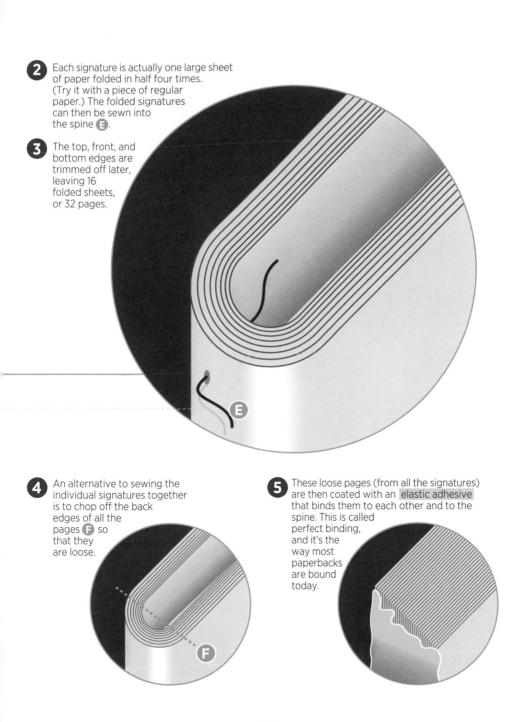

E

4 An alternative to sewing the individual signatures together is to chop off the back edges of all the pages **F** so that they are loose.

F

5 These loose pages (from all the signatures) are then coated with an elastic adhesive that binds them to each other and to the spine. This is called perfect binding, and it's the way most paperbacks are bound today.

Travel writer

You travel. Why not write about it?
Long-time Lonely Planet author and
editor Don George offers five key
tenets to get you started.

1 Exude respect

It is essential that you respect the history,
creations, and beliefs of the places and
peoples that you encounter. Don't
disparage or diminish them. Honour
them, and that honour will be returned
to you. And that will enable you to unlock
the key to their heart.

2 Know before you go

Study the background of the places and
peoples you're visiting before you arrive.
Know their history, culture, art, and
spiritual beliefs. That knowledge will
provide context, connections, and layers
for all your discoveries on the ground.

Pursue your passion

Always look for your passion point in a place. Let's say you love puppets and you're going to Paris. Then seek out the Parisian master puppeteer and visit him in his workshop. You'll discover a passion-piece of Paris that's yours alone.

Embrace serendipity

You're planning to go to famous festival A. But then you meet a local who says, "Festival A has become so touristy. You should go to Festival B. Only the locals know about it and it's amazing." Embrace the opportunity and make the detour to Festival B. You'll have a better experience and get a better story.

5 Read, read, read

Of course you have to travel and write to be a travel writer. But you also have to read. Read the travel lit classics and the contemporary masters. Read fiction set in the places you're visiting. Analyse what makes great writing soar and apply those lessons to your own fledgling prose.

Professional blogger

It seems as though everybody's got a blog. How can you join in and also stand out from the crowd?

MY VERY

❶ Choose a platform ...

There are many blogging platforms, and **many of them are free.** Blogger and Wordpress are both well-established and free. You might opt for a paid site if you're looking for serious flexibility and all the trimmings.

❷ and a topic

You need to have something to say. Chances are if you write about **something that you are deeply interested in**, you'll find others that share your passion. You need to build a fan base if you're going to make a living from this.

❸ Start a fan base, and make it grow!

The quality of your writing, images, video, quizzes ... whatever it is you're producing, has to be good. But no matter how good it is, you're going to need to work at getting it out there.

For instance, you could:

● Begin with **your own social networks** and refer friends and family to your blog

● **Join a forum** that is related to your blog topic. Get to know the forum and its members. They might like what you have to say.

...IG BLOG

④ Doing the work

Writing a blog means you need to ... **write!** And if you want people to spread the word about your blog, it will need to be of a certain quality. Basic grammar, spelling ... it makes a difference.

● Writing doesn't come naturally for everyone, but the most important thing is to **write in your own words** — don't try and write in a style that is not the way you speak.

● Keep it **simple.**

● **Spell check!**

● If there's someone whose opinions you trust, maybe **have your posts read through** before you publish — even if it's just to make sure that everything makes sense.

⑤ Turning a blog into money

There are a few ways you can make money from your blog:

● Get on **affiliate programs** and recommend products that are sold through them. Like books — if there are books you think would be relevant to your audience, link to an online bookseller and join their affiliate sales program

● **"Adsense"** Carry contextualised ads on your site served by Google.

● **Get paid for your content** If you really hit the mark with your writing you might get approached to do some professional writing for other sites or publications.

HOW TO BE AN ...

Interpreter ... or a translator

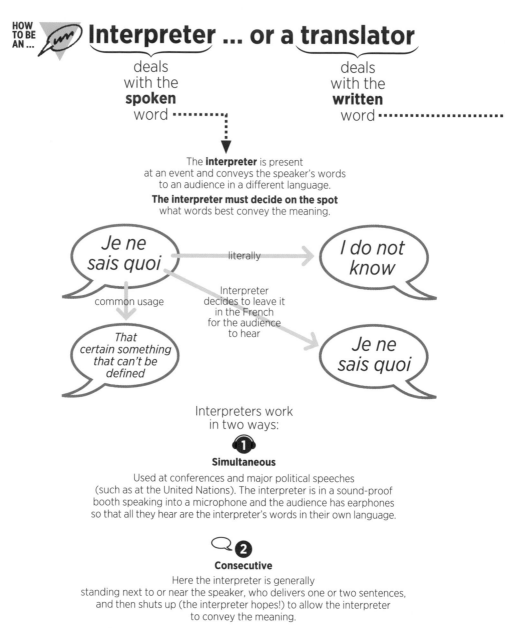

Interpreter deals with the **spoken** word ....

translator deals with the **written** word ....

The **interpreter** is present at an event and conveys the speaker's words to an audience in a different language. **The interpreter must decide on the spot** what words best convey the meaning.

Je ne sais quoi

literally → *I do not know*

common usage → *That certain something that can't be defined*

Interpreter decides to leave it in the French for the audience to hear → *Je ne sais quoi*

Interpreters work in two ways:

① Simultaneous

Used at conferences and major political speeches (such as at the United Nations). The interpreter is in a sound-proof booth speaking into a microphone and the audience has earphones so that all they hear are the interpreter's words in their own language.

② Consecutive

Here the interpreter is generally standing next to or near the speaker, who delivers one or two sentences, and then shuts up (the interpreter hopes!) to allow the interpreter to convey the meaning.

Interpreters (on phones) are employed in stores or hospitals where a shopper or patient doesn't know the language and needs help. It's a much cheaper, although much less personal, alternative to having a person walking around helping people.

The **translator** is seldom present
when a writer is writing.

So, unlike interpreting, translation is used where anything written,
for instance, business and legal documents, can be read by someone
who doesn't know the language.

Also unlike an interpreter, a translator can make extensive use of
computer programs in the preparation of a translated text.
The main constraint is the deadline!

An important aspect of the job is the translation of non-fiction and fiction —
in some cases, the great works of literature.

When it went wrong ... or did it?

Don't believe the "I am a doughnut" story!

 A popular case of misinterpretation involved John F. Kennedy's
famous speech in Berlin on June 26th, 1963, when he expressed solidarity
with the people of West Berlin by declaring
"Ich bin ein Berliner!"
In parts of Germany, Berliner means jelly doughnut,
and in the years that followed the speech the idea grew that
the president had declared himself to be a pastry.
In fact his grammar was tip-top, but it's such a delicious story,
it won't go away!

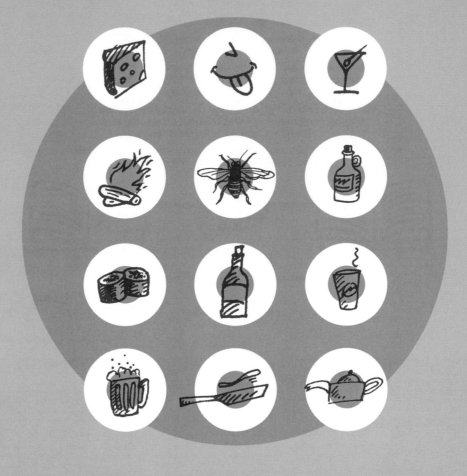

FOOD AND DRINK

Cheesemaker

Cheesemaking is not that complicated; it's all in the details—details that can produce a huge variety of tastes (and smells!). Estimates vary for how many different cheeses there are in the world, ranging from 500 to 1,000.

Let's look at just one of them: **cheddar.**

The milk

● There are two main breeds of milking cow. Many cheesemakers like **Brown Swiss** cows ( ) because they produce protein-rich milk, and they continue to produce it for longer than the average **Holstein** — the classic picture-book cow ( ).

● **The quality of the milk depends on what the cows eat.** Fresh pasture with a mixture of grasses and legumes is best. Here are three **legumes** that the Brown Swiss love:

clover

alfafa

timothy

The process

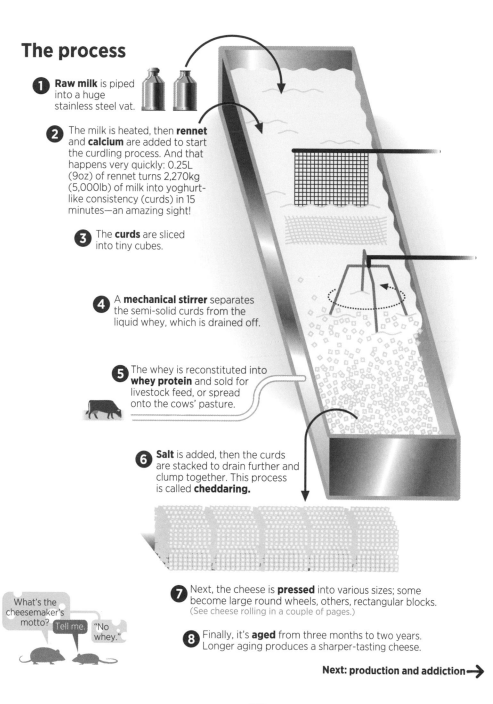

1 **Raw milk** is piped into a huge stainless steel vat.

2 The milk is heated, then **rennet** and **calcium** are added to start the curdling process. And that happens very quickly: 0.25L (9oz) of rennet turns 2,270kg (5,000lb) of milk into yoghurt-like consistency (curds) in 15 minutes—an amazing sight!

3 The **curds** are sliced into tiny cubes.

4 A **mechanical stirrer** separates the semi-solid curds from the liquid whey, which is drained off.

5 The whey is reconstituted into **whey protein** and sold for livestock feed, or spread onto the cows' pasture.

6 **Salt** is added, then the curds are stacked to drain further and clump together. This process is called **cheddaring.**

What's the cheesemaker's motto? *Tell me.* "No whey."

7 Next, the cheese is **pressed** into various sizes; some become large round wheels, others, rectangular blocks. (See cheese rolling in a couple of pages.)

8 Finally, it's **aged** from three months to two years. Longer aging produces a sharper-tasting cheese.

Next: production and addiction→

Cheesy animals
It's not just cows, of course.

From **cows** and **goats**
you get

1

kilogram
(2.2lb)
of cheese

from every

10

litres
(2.6gal)
of milk.

From **sheep**
you get

1

kilogram
(2.2lb)
of cheese

from every

6

litres
(1.6gal)
of milk.

So sheep's milk
cheese is much richer.

Camel's milk
is made into cheese
dry desert areas o
Africa and the Mido
East. The milk has
enough nutrients t
sustain a person
throughout the da

This milk is good fe
people with lactos
intolerance, and ha
lower cholesterol th
other animals' mil

They make
cheese from
camel's milk
in Mauritania.
They call it
Camelbert.

Why we ♥ cheese
Don't worry, you can't help it.

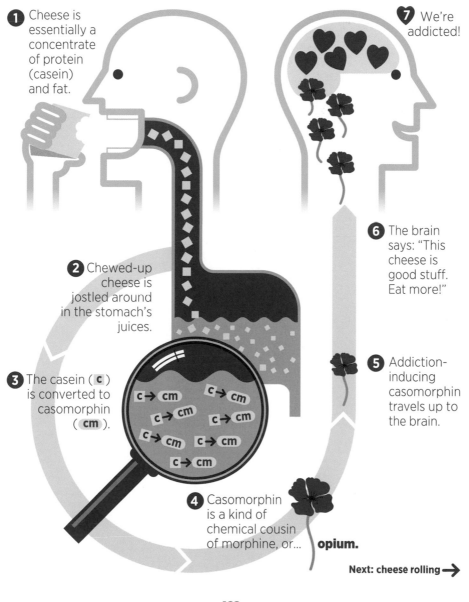

1 Cheese is essentially a concentrate of protein (casein) and fat.

2 Chewed-up cheese is jostled around in the stomach's juices.

3 The casein (**c**) is converted to casomorphin (**cm**).

c→cm c→cm
c→cm c→cm
c→cm c→cm
c→cm

4 Casomorphin is a kind of chemical cousin of morphine, or... **opium.**

5 Addiction-inducing casomorphin travels up to the brain.

6 The brain says: "This cheese is good stuff. Eat more!"

7 We're addicted!

Next: cheese rolling →

Cheese rolling!

Really. They do it in England.

Cheese rolling has taken place in England since the 15th century.

The modern event is held every spring at Cooper's Hill, Brockhurst, in Gloucestershire.

1 Foolhardy contestants line up.

2 The **Official Roller** pushes the cheese down the hill, with a second or two head start before the runners go.

3 This part of the hill is not visible from the top.

4 The cheese is a **Double Gloucester** wheel weighing 4kg (9lb).

International cheese rollers!

It's not just another totally English oddity; in 2014 an Australian won one of the races. And in the past, Japanese and American contestants have won races.

5 As the cheese rolls down the hill it can reach **112km/h (70mph).** Because of the danger to spectators, it was replaced by a foam replica in 2013.

6 There are **four downhill races** (three for men, one for women) and uphill races for boys and girls under 14 (no cheese involved).

If cheese throwing isn't silly enough for you, try

Rat throwing!
Really. They do it in Spain.

In the centuries-old tradition of **San Pedro Nolasco,** people in El Puig smash *cuañas,* which are like piñatas, but made of clay. Half of the *cuañas* are filled with dead rats, the rest with candy. The rats are then thrown at the crowd. A *Batalla de Ratas* ensues.

Madrid
El Puig
Valencia

Not content with hurling **dead rats,** which is officially banned but still takes place every January, Spaniards also have festivals for throwing:

flour & eggs
tomatoes
black tar
flowers
grapes
water

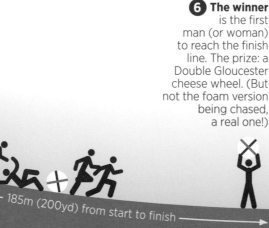

6 **The winner** is the first man (or woman) to reach the finish line. The prize: a Double Gloucester cheese wheel. (But not the foam version being chased, a real one!)

7 **Ambulances** wait to ferry injured runners to the local hospital. There are several accidents every year.

185m (200yd) from start to finish

Food taster

Actually, the sensation we experience when we eat is a combo of taste, smell, texture, temperature and "hotness," but food critics agree that taste is the important thing.)

There are five areas of the tongue where specific tastes are sensed by our taste buds
(of which there are 10,000!)

Sensations from any part of the tongue can blend to form subtle variations.

1 Bitterness
things like: kale, endive, radicchio, coffee, beer, tonic water

2 Sourness
lemon, grapefruit, pickles, alcohol, sour cream

3 Savouriness (Umami)
beef, bacon, parmesan cheese, miso, MSG, seaweed

4 Saltiness
soy, capers, olives, pork, anchovies, sea vegetables

5 Sweetness
honey, molasses, fruit, cinnamon, chocolate, sweets (+ sugar!).

The correctness, or usefulness of the "tongue map" (first drawn in 1901) has been questioned since the 1970s—not the taste sensations, just where they appear on the tongue. But we like maps, so there.

Quite apart from the taste of the food itself, If you want to be a critic, consider where and how the meal is served.

A good food critic will cover these criteria:

- **Service:** Polite? Knowlegeable? There when you want it and NOT when you don't?
- **Noise level:** Conversation possible, or sore throat the next day?
- **Price:** Reasonable for what you ate?

Wear a disguise.

Only necessary when you have become a celebrity food critic. A wig, perhaps or a false moustache (watch the soup!).

And you must go more than once.

The head chef might have been away, or a waitperson didn't show up for work, or those kids at the next table wouldn't stop shouting at each other.
One drawback: going more than once means you'll need more than one disguise. But then dressing up might make **eating out every night** bearable!

HOW TO BE A ... Mixologist

Make me a martini! (Please.) These days a brave mixologist will mix it up—so tequila or practically any strong alcohol can stand in for gin or vodka, updating the classic cocktail. Some ideas:

Basic method

1 Fill cocktail glass with ice and water. Let it stand while you continue.

2 Fill shaker with ice.

3 Measure ingredients and pour into shaker.

4 Shake with passion. Shake again. Shake until the ice is broken into tiny shards.

5 Throw ice and water out of the glass, and pour the mix in. Three-part shakers have a built-in strainer, but if there's fruit (or other solids) in the mix, use a separate, fine strainer.

Martinis   Shot = 30mL (1oz)

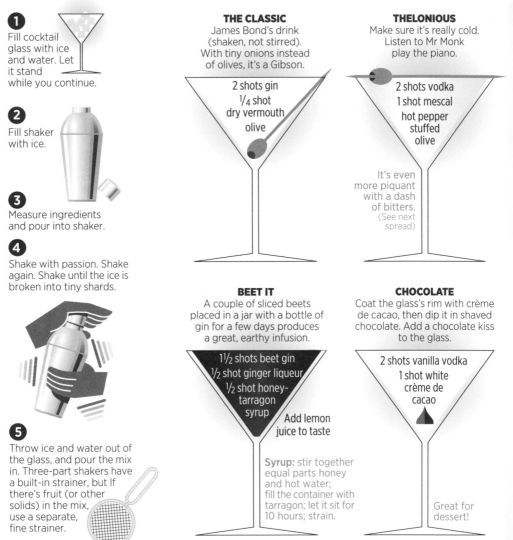

THE CLASSIC
James Bond's drink (shaken, not stirred). With tiny onions instead of olives, it's a Gibson.

2 shots gin
1/4 shot dry vermouth
olive

THELONIOUS
Make sure it's really cold. Listen to Mr Monk play the piano.

2 shots vodka
1 shot mescal
hot pepper stuffed olive

It's even more piquant with a dash of bitters. (See next spread)

BEET IT
A couple of sliced beets placed in a jar with a bottle of gin for a few days produces a great, earthy infusion.

1 1/2 shots beet gin
1/2 shot ginger liqueur
1/2 shot honey-tarragon syrup

Add lemon juice to taste

Syrup: stir together equal parts honey and hot water; fill the container with tarragon; let it sit for 10 hours; strain.

CHOCOLATE
Coat the glass's rim with crème de cacao, then dip it in shaved chocolate. Add a chocolate kiss to the glass.

2 shots vanilla vodka
1 shot white crème de cacao

Great for dessert!

138

Other cocktails to try

HOP, SKIP AND GO NAKED

Despite the odd combination, this is surprisingly tasty and refreshing. Beware: one is probably enough!

In a beer glass filled with ice put:

1 shot vodka
1 shot gin
splash of lime juice
fill glass with beer

CAMBUCA

A little weird, but peculiarly tasty.

½ shot Campari
½ shot sambuca

FERNET AND COKE

While Fernet is traditionally what you take that dreadful morning after a hearty party, this popular drink from Argentina is a way to prolong the party itself.

Combine the first three ingredients in a large ice-filled glass and stir. Strain into an ice-filled tumbler. Fill up with soda.

Coke reduction: boil a bottle of Coca-Cola until half the original amount remains. Allow to cool. Keep in the fridge.

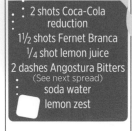

2 shots Coca-Cola reduction
1½ shots Fernet Branca
¼ shot lemon juice
2 dashes Angostura Bitters
(See next spread)
soda water
lemon zest

How to impress drinking buddies with mixology

The amazing POUSSE CAFÉ

This works on the principle that some liquids are more dense than others. Thicker, heavier liquids go in first, and each succeeding one floats on top of the one before it.

Pour each liquid slowly over a teaspoon held bottom side up and just touching the inside of the glass.

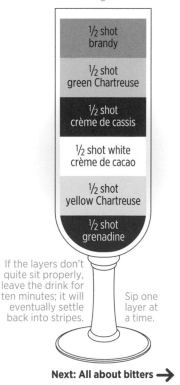

½ shot brandy

½ shot green Chartreuse

½ shot crème de cassis

½ shot white crème de cacao

½ shot yellow Chartreuse

½ shot grenadine

If the layers don't quite sit properly, leave the drink for ten minutes; it will eventually settle back into stripes.

Sip one layer at a time.

Next: All about bitters →

Bitters: essential again

Once widely used by bartenders, bitters fell out of fashion. With the return to a new era of cocktails, bitters are becoming a new staple in bars, incorporated again in classic drinks as well as new concoctions.

1 shot = 30mL (1oz)

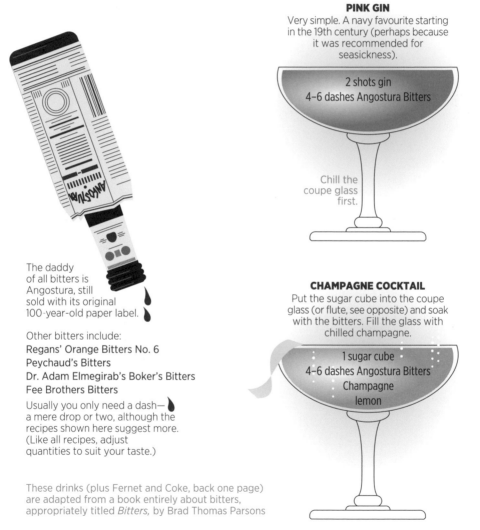

The daddy of all bitters is Angostura, still sold with its original 100-year-old paper label.

Other bitters include:
Regans' Orange Bitters No. 6
Peychaud's Bitters
Dr. Adam Elmegirab's Boker's Bitters
Fee Brothers Bitters

Usually you only need a dash— a mere drop or two, although the recipes shown here suggest more. (Like all recipes, adjust quantities to suit your taste.)

These drinks (plus Fernet and Coke, back one page) are adapted from a book entirely about bitters, appropriately titled *Bitters*, by Brad Thomas Parsons

PINK GIN

Very simple. A navy favourite starting in the 19th century (perhaps because it was recommended for seasickness).

2 shots gin
4–6 dashes Angostura Bitters

Chill the coupe glass first.

CHAMPAGNE COCKTAIL

Put the sugar cube into the coupe glass (or flute, see opposite) and soak with the bitters. Fill the glass with chilled champagne.

1 sugar cube
4–6 dashes Angostura Bitters
Champagne
lemon

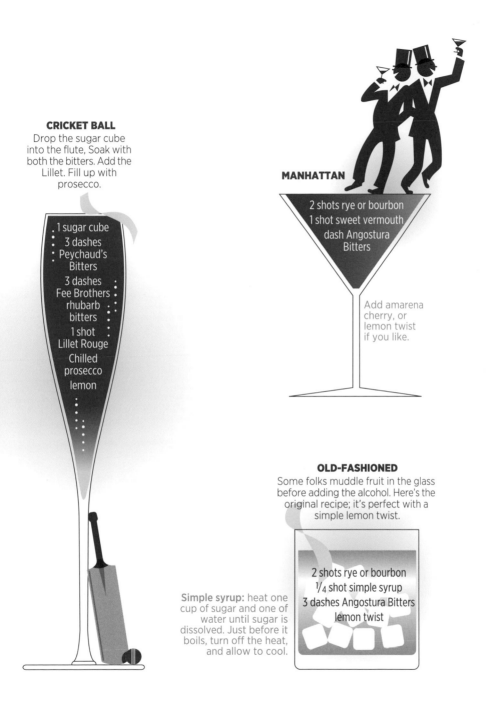

CRICKET BALL

Drop the sugar cube into the flute, Soak with both the bitters. Add the Lillet. Fill up with prosecco.

1 sugar cube

3 dashes Peychaud's Bitters

3 dashes Fee Brothers rhubarb bitters

1 shot Lillet Rouge

Chilled prosecco

lemon

MANHATTAN

2 shots rye or bourbon

1 shot sweet vermouth

dash Angostura Bitters

Add amarena cherry, or lemon twist if you like.

OLD-FASHIONED

Some folks muddle fruit in the glass before adding the alcohol. Here's the original recipe; it's perfect with a simple lemon twist.

2 shots rye or bourbon

$1/4$ shot simple syrup

3 dashes Angostura Bitters

lemon twist

Simple syrup: heat one cup of sugar and one of water until sugar is dissolved. Just before it boils, turn off the heat, and allow to cool.

Maori cook

The traditional Maori way to cook food is in a hangi. In New Zealand nowadays it's typically reserved for special occasions, but the method shown here goes back at least two thousand years, and it's still used in Chile and parts of Africa.

Here's what you'll need

- large stones
- 1 cubic metre of firewood
- kindling (to get it started)
- meat
- vegetables
- chickenwire baskets (the kids can make these; you'll need chickenwire, pliers ... and sticking-plasters)
- cloths, sheets, hessian sacks
- large bucket of water
- shovels, rakes
- heavy duty gloves (to protect hands while lifting the wire baskets out of the pit)
- strong friends to help dig the hole
- beer (lots)

The whole thing takes about six hours, so **LET'S GET GOING!**

1 BUILD A FIRE

Cover an area 1m (about 3ft) square with large river stones. Make sure you are about 3m (nearly 10ft) from any structure, foliage, drains or septic tanks.

Place kindling, then a stack of logs on top of the stones and light the fire. Keep feeding the pile of wood for **two to three hours** so that the stones get white hot.

Stones can explode when heated, so it's a good idea to do a test run—heat them up—24 hours before the event to make sure you're using the right type of stones.

(You can use iron bars instead of stones; you'll need to get these red hot.)

It's thirsty work. Have a beer. Or two.

2 DIG A PIT

While the stones are heating up, dig a hole **1m (3ft) deep and 1m square,** near the fire.

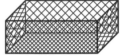

3 MAKE THE WIRE BASKETS

This'll keep the young ones busy, while you are digging. The aim is just to contain the food when it's in the pit; so the baskets can be very simply constructed.

← about 0.5m (1.6ft) →

4 PREPARE THE FOOD

Wrap the meat and veggies [in] old, wet tea towels or other clean cloths, and place them [in] the wire baskets.

Put the meat in and veggies in separate cloths.

You might want to line the baskets with tinfoil; this will ensure none of the earth or [?] from the pit gets mixed up with the food.

⑤ HOT STONES INTO THE PIT

When the stones, or iron bars are hot—that'll take two hours or a bit more with the fire on top of them—pull the wood aside, and drag the stones or bars into the pit with rakes. (Leave them in the fire longer if they aren't *really, really* hot.)

This would not be a good time to fall into the pit.

⑥ START COOKING

So as not to lose heat, put the wire baskets with the bundles of food inside into the pit as quickly as you can. The meat-filled baskets should go in first, then the vegetables.

top layer: veg
bottom: meat

⑦ COVER THE FOOD

Lay old sheets on top of the baskets, then the hessian sacks.

sacks
sheets

⑧ POUR WATER ON IT

A large bucketful.

⑨ STEAM!

Pouring water on the hot stones will produce **a lot** of steam.  **Caution:** if you get burned by the steam, flush the wound with cold water.

Quickly shovel the pile of earth from the pit back into it to trap as much of the steam as possible. No-one wants half-cooked meat.

⑩ WAIT

Could it possibly be time for another...?

Cheers! When do we eat?

Here's to the hangi!

⑪ THREE HOURS LATER...

Dig the whole thing up. Take care not to stick your shovel into the wire baskets.

⑫ FINALLY! UNWRAP AND EAT

If you've timed it right, by now the sun is probably setting, so no-one can tell if some of the food is a bit raw anyway. And, you guessed, beer goes really well with it.

POSTSCRIPT ☽
Once dark, it's traditional for a few people to stumble into the pit. Please leave the sacks and cloths on the now-cold stones to break their fall.

 # Beekeeper

Bees pollinate 80% of flowering crops, and that's about one-third of everything we eat. But bees are under attack by Colony Collapse Disorder, a disease that's reducing bee populations around the world.

So beekeeping is important. (Of course it is!—why do you think I'm in this book?)
Here's how to get going:

1 FIND A COURSE TO TAKE
Colleges and universities that specialise in agriculture are a good place to start: they'll have links to further education courses and local beekeepers and beekeeping clubs.

2 DO RESEARCH
There are lots of books about beekeeping. You can also search the web for information.

3 BUY OR BUILD A HIVE
Lots of parts!

Waterproof outer cover

Inner cover

"Super" (more of these can be added)
Worker bees make honey here

Queen excluder
Worker bees can pass through

Brood chamber
Queen lays eggs here

Entrance block (for bees)

Hive stand

 Old-fashioned hives (called "skeps") were made of straw.

④ GET OTHER EQUIPMENT

You'll need:

- **hive tool** acting as a lever, loosens honeycomb frames and boxes.
- **uncapping knife** cuts the top off wax cells during harvesting.
- **smoker** calms the bees when you open a hive to remove honeycombs.

⑤ PROTECT YOURSELF

There are full beekeeping suits, but you can use your own clothes. Just make sure they are light-coloured and tucked into socks (and into your gloves). One thing you should buy is a proper helmet with a veil or plastic visor over your face.

⑥ BUY BEES!

They usually come in packages from local beekeepers. Contents will vary, but here's what you might expect, drawn actual size:

up to **10,000 worker bees** 1.3kg (3lb)	about **300 drones**	**1 queen bee**
Lifespan: 6–7 weeks	4 months The only reason to be in the hive is to mate with the queen. (Then they die.)	3–4 years

Next: Honey →

Making honey

Not to put too fine a point on it, but honey starts out as bee-vomit.

① COLLECTING NECTAR

Forager bees collect nectar from flowering plants.

Forager bees regurgitate nectar into **processor bees.**

It's stored in the "honey stomach".

(Forager flies off for more nectar.)

② FILLING THE HONEYCOMB

Processor bees go into the hive and regurgitate the nectar into a wax cell.

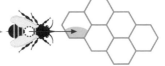

Both the honey and the cells are made of processed nectar. Bees make the cells hexagonal because that's the strongest and most space-efficient shape.

③ DRYING THE NECTAR

Honey is about 18% water but nectar is 70%, so bees must dry it out by fanning their wings to create an airflow around the honeycomb.

70%

18%

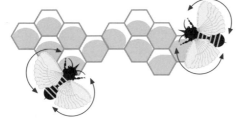

④ CAPPING THE CELLS

When the nectar in the cells has ripened and evaporated, it becomes thick, sweet honey. Bees then cap the cells with more of the nectar from their stomachs, and it hardens into wax.

⑤ HARVESTING THE HONEY, 1

You don't have to destroy the honeycomb to gather honey. (This is a big relief to the bees who spent many hours making it.) First you must scrape off the outer wax coating (see ④) with the uncapping knife.

Some knives have electric heating coils.

⑥ HARVESTING, 2

Scraped honeycomb frames are placed in a centrifuge machine which spins the honey out of the cells. The comb is returned to the hive and the bees get to work again.

What to do if you get stung (and you probably will)

- Pull the stinger out.
- Take an ibuprofen or acetaminophen tablet to relieve the pain.
- Wash with soap and water.
- Hold an ice-pack to the site for about 20 minutes. Relief should last for about 5 hours; re-ice if the pain comes back.
- Other home remedies include damp pastes of baking soda, toothpaste, raw onion or potato; calamine lotion; hydrocortisone cream; deodorant; even honey!
- **IMPORTANT:** If you start to have an allergic reaction, seek medical help immediately.

Not all bees sting— just females, and they usually die afer the deed—but they'll only attack you if threatened. This is why you need a smoker (previous page) when moving parts of the hive.

What's on the menu?

Bees visit whatever flowers they can find and then naturally blend the gathered pollen and nectar.
Try these in your garden:

- **Spring:** crocus, hyacinth, borage, calendula, wild lilac
- **Summer:** cosmos, echinacea, snapdragons, foxgloves, hosta
- **Late summer:** zinnias, sedum, asters, witch hazel, goldenrod

What else do bees pollinate? (Told you they were important!)

Apart from bees, other insects, birds, rain and wind are all pollinators, but bees are the most important. Here are the percentages of a some of the crops pollinated by bees.

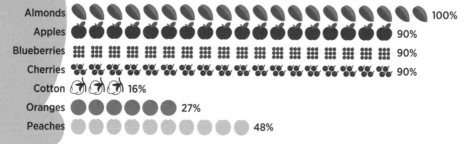

Almonds	100%
Apples	90%
Blueberries	90%
Cherries	90%
Cotton	16%
Oranges	27%
Peaches	48%

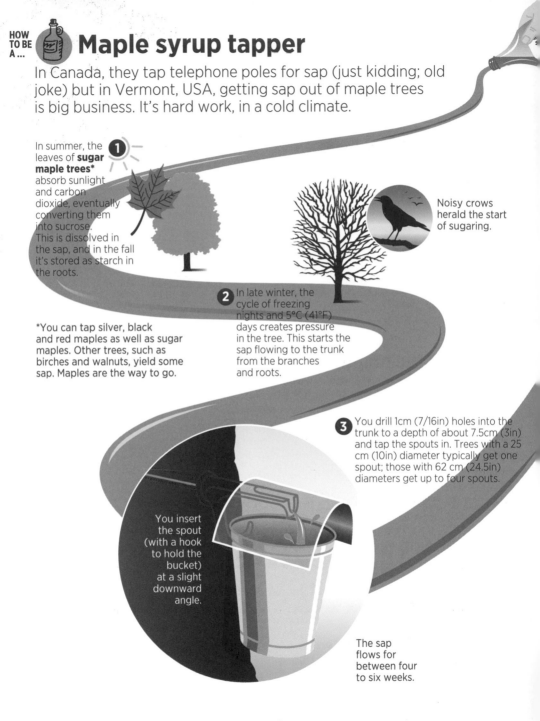

Maple syrup tapper

HOW TO BE A...

In Canada, they tap telephone poles for sap (just kidding; old joke) but in Vermont, USA, getting sap out of maple trees is big business. It's hard work, in a cold climate.

1 In summer, the leaves of **sugar maple trees*** absorb sunlight and carbon dioxide, eventually converting them into sucrose. This is dissolved in the sap, and in the fall it's stored as starch in the roots.

Noisy crows herald the start of sugaring.

*You can tap silver, black and red maples as well as sugar maples. Other trees, such as birches and walnuts, yield some sap. Maples are the way to go.

2 In late winter, the cycle of freezing nights and 5°C (41°F) days creates pressure in the tree. This starts the sap flowing to the trunk from the branches and roots.

3 You drill 1cm (7/16in) holes into the trunk to a depth of about 7.5cm (3in) and tap the spouts in. Trees with a 25 cm (10in) diameter typically get one spout; those with 62 cm (24.5in) diameters get up to four spouts.

You insert the spout (with a hook to hold the bucket) at a slight downward angle.

The sap flows for between four to six weeks.

5 Some maple syrupers still use horses to drag the collecting tank to the sugarhouse ...

others bypass this stage by attaching plastic tubes to the spouts on the trees and letting gravity transfer the sap directly from the tree to the sugarhouse.

4 The buckets of sap are poured into a collecting tank.

6 In the sugarhouse, sap flows into the evaporator, where water is burned off, leaving syrup. On average, 150L (40 gallons) of sap makes about 3.5L (1 gallon) of syrup.

Some sugar maples have produced sap for centuries.

Yes, you can still see marks left by the spouts.

7 The sound of woodpeckers drumming against the galvanized collecting buckets marks the end of the season. It's time to take the spouts out (gently, so the trees heal) and wait for another year.

Sushi maker

Sushi was first eaten in Japan in the 8th century. At first sushi was a way to preserve fish in fermented rice. Later, people started eating the rice as well. In the 19th century, sushi became the original fast food. But you don't have to travel to Japan to roll with the sushi experts.

1 **Make sushi rice.**

- Wash the short grain or "sushi" rice. It can be white or brown.

- Cover rice with water and bring to boil, then turn heat down and cover. Cook for 6 to 8 minutes.

- While it's cooking, heat rice vinegar, sugar and salt until the sugar dissolves.

- Put cooked rice in a large bowl; add vinegar mixture and fold together.

- To keep the texture, use soon. Don't refrigerate, it will harden the rice.

2 Use a **bamboo sushi-rolling mat.**

3 Add a **sheet of nori,** rough side up. Then put a handful of rice on top ...

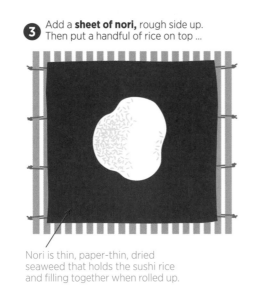

Nori is thin, paper-thin, dried seaweed that holds the sushi rice and filling together when rolled up.

4 and **spread it evenly,** 1.25cm (0.5in) thick. Leave 2.5cm (1in) all round.

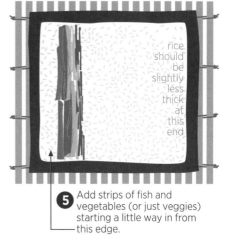

rice should be slightly less thick at this end

5 Add strips of fish and vegetables (or just veggies) starting a little way in from this edge.

6 **Roll up tightly,** squeezing as you go.

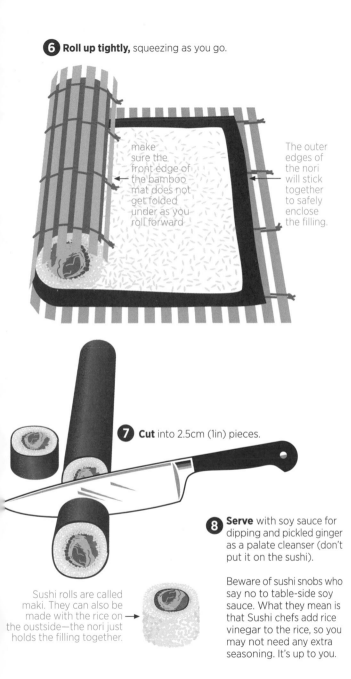

make sure the front edge of the bamboo mat does not get folded under as you roll forward

The outer edges of the nori will stick together to safely enclose the filling.

7 **Cut** into 2.5cm (1in) pieces.

Sushi rolls are called maki. They can also be made with the rice on the outside—the nori just holds the filling together.

8 **Serve** with soy sauce for dipping and pickled ginger as a palate cleanser (don't put it on the sushi).

Beware of sushi snobs who say no to table-side soy sauce. What they mean is that Sushi chefs add rice vinegar to the rice, so you may not need any extra seasoning. It's up to you.

Inside story

You can put almost anything into a roll. Here are some traditional choices:

sliced vegetables
- carrots
- cucumber
- scallions
- avocado
- spicy pickles
- cooked spinach
- shitake mushrooms
- sweet potato

raw fish
- tuna
- salmon

cooked fish
- sliced tuna steaks
- shrimp
- crabmeat

Translating the the menu when you decide to go out and let someone else make the sushi

shake	fresh salmon
maguro	bluefin tuna
hamachi	yellowfin tuna
toro	fatty tuna
ebi	cooked shrimp
unagi	grilled freshwater eel
tai	red snapper
kani	crabmeat
tamago	sweet egg custard wrapped in dried seaweed
tempura	fish or veggies dipped in batter and deep fried
uni	sea urchin
wasabi	Japanese horseradish

Sommelier

Want to help diners navigate an intimidating wine list? Apply here. The idea is to match wines to the diners' chosen food, at a price they like.

❶ Know your wine

You won't go through this routine ⟶ at every table (especially the spitty bit), but you should taste every wine on the list that diners are choosing from. And yes, you will spit it out when you have to try 10 wines in one tasting. Then another 10 ...

❷ Buzzwords

The words that wine snobs use to describe a wine's taste or its "bouquet" (that's one of those words, right there) can leave diners baffled or, more likely, annoyed. Use simple descriptive language and your customers will get a good idea of what they are going to drink.

After a smell, a swirl and a sip, **see if any of these match the experience:**
CRISP fresh, grassy
ACIDIC tart
BUTTERY creamy, round, oaky
FULL-BODIED bold, lots of flavour
SPICY black pepper
SMOKY burnt
EARTHY barnyard
SWEET honey
FRUITY blackcurrant, raspberry, apple, etc.
YESS! I like it! (my favourite)

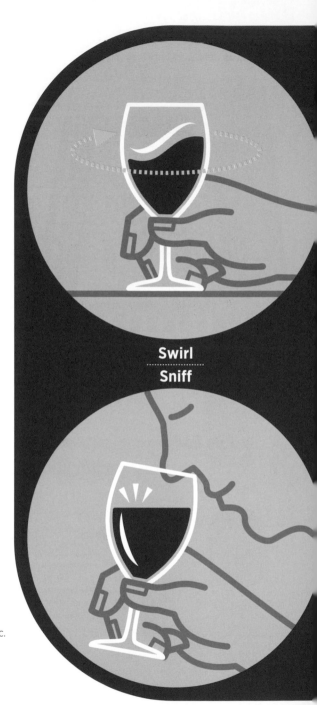

Swirl
Sniff

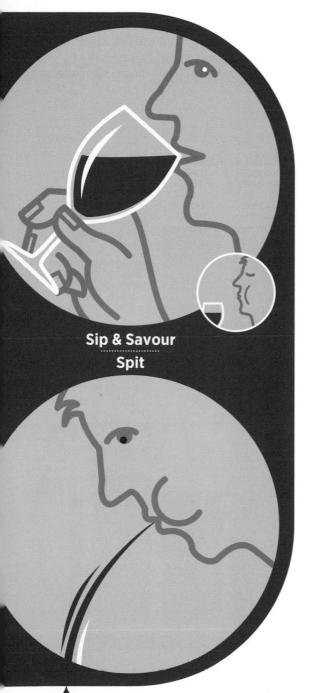

Sip & Savour

Spit

❸ Pairing

Most diners pick their food first and then think about what to drink with it. Here are the basic rules about **what goes with what.**

CHINESE CUISINE	sweet white
FRENCH	light red/rich white
INDIAN	sweet white/rose
ITALIAN	medium red
SPANISH	medium red
THAI	sweet white

SALTY FOOD	sparkling
CHICKEN	light red/dry white
FISH	dry white
SHELLFISH	rich white
CREAMY PASTA	rich white
RISOTTO	light red
PORKCHOPS	light red
DUCK	medium red
ROASTED MEAT	bold red
SMOKED MEAT	bold red
BARBEQUE	bold red
VEGETABLES	dry white
PIZZA	medium red

But "rules" are made to be broken. A good sommelier will suggest, and then let diners drink what tastes good to them!

Barista

A barista operates the espresso machine in a coffee shop.

Fun fact: the bar is the pressure rating on most espresso machines (usually it's 135 lb/sq in) but it isn't where the word barista comes from—it means bartender in Italian

HOW TO BE A ...

Know your drinks!

1

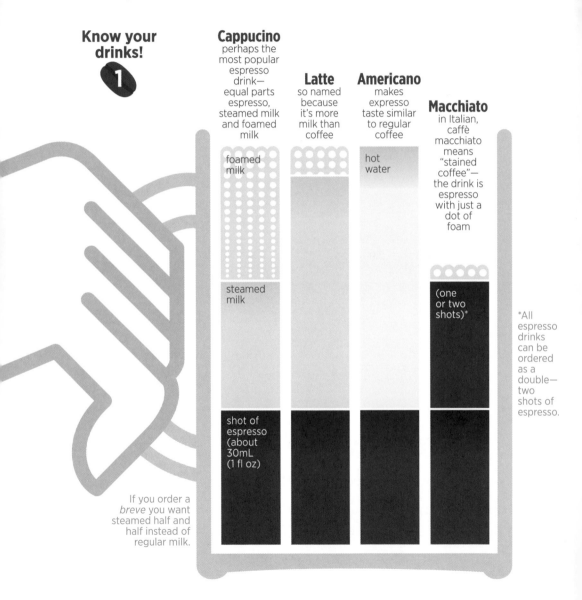

Cappucino perhaps the most popular espresso drink— equal parts espresso, steamed milk and foamed milk

foamed milk

steamed milk

shot of espresso (about 30mL (1 fl oz)

Latte so named because it's more milk than coffee

Americano makes expresso taste similar to regular coffee

hot water

Macchiato in Italian, caffè macchiato means "stained coffee"— the drink is espresso with just a dot of foam

(one or two shots)*

*All espresso drinks can be ordered as a double— two shots of espresso.

If you order a *breve* you want steamed half and half instead of regular milk.

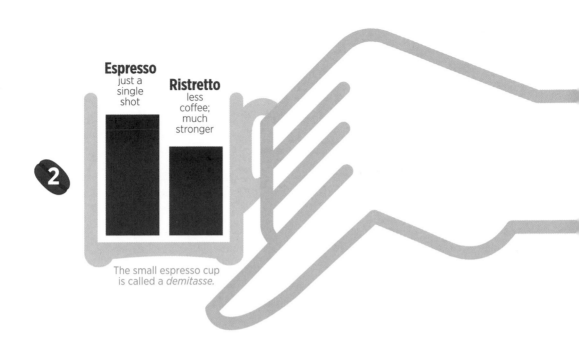

Espresso
just a single shot

Ristretto
less coffee; much stronger

2

The small espresso cup is called a *demitasse*.

Making coffee without going out for it

You can buy fairly decent, small versions of the professional espresso machines you see in coffee shops, but there are other ways to be a home barista.

Stove-top espresso

Water is boiled in the lower part, forced up a tube then it flows down through finely ground beans.

Filter

Finely ground beans are placed into a paper or reusable plastic cone, and boiling water poured over it. While grounds stay in the cone, the coffee is ready to drink.

Plunger

Boiling water is poured over coarsely ground beans. After a few minutes, the plunger is pushed to the bottom of the pot, trapping the grounds while you pour the coffee.

Percolator

Credited with civilising America's Wild West, a coffee percolator boils water, sending it up through a tube and down over coarsely ground beans held in a metal filter at the top.

Brewer

Beer is one of the oldest drinks produced by humans. Chemical tests of jars from 3500 BC found in modern-day Iran, show traces of brewed ale. Over time, brewing has moved from those first artisinal efforts through mass production starting in the Industrial Revolution, and recently back to microbreweries producing special ales and lagers.

Here's the basic process

1 **Grain** is crushed in a mill ...

2 and mixed with hot water. Grain adds starch and flavour. The result (called "mash") is like hot cereal.

3 The liquid part of the mix ("wort") is drained and transferred to a large kettle where it's cooked at a rolling boil.

4 The brewer adds **hops** for flavour and aroma.

5 It's all transferred to stainless-steel fermenting tanks and chilled. Then **yeast** is added. This converts sugars in the mixture to alcohol and carbon dioxide.

Where to start your brewing business: the 10 b(eer)est countries

The amount of beer drunk per person there in 2012, in **litres** (gallons)

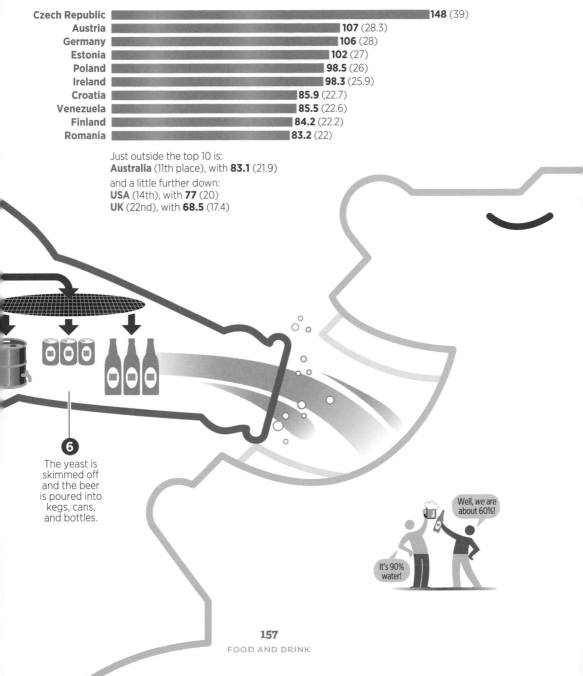

Country	litres (gallons)
Czech Republic	**148** (39)
Austria	**107** (28.3)
Germany	**106** (28)
Estonia	**102** (27)
Poland	**98.5** (26)
Ireland	**98.3** (25.9)
Croatia	**85.9** (22.7)
Venezuela	**85.5** (22.6)
Finland	**84.2** (22.2)
Romania	**83.2** (22)

Just outside the top 10 is:
Australia (11th place), with **83.1** (21.9)

and a little further down:
USA (14th), with **77** (20)
UK (22nd), with **68.5** (17.4)

6
The yeast is skimmed off and the beer is poured into kegs, cans, and bottles.

It's 90% water!

Well, *we* are about 60%!

 **Crêpier**

Let's start with a good recipe.

You'll need these ...

- 500ml (1pt) milk
- 3 eggs, beaten
- 1 cup of flour
- 1 1/2 teaspoons of sugar
- 1/8 teaspoon of salt
- 2 tablespoons of butter, melted

to make the batter

1 Put the flour in a bowl and make a well in the centre.

2 Add the milk slowly, whisking it in as you go.

3 Whisk in the beaten egg, then the butter.

4 Add the salt and sugar, whisk to combine.

Some fillings

- berries of all kinds
- apples
- peaches
- rhubarb
- bananas
- jam
- peanut butter
- mascarpone cheese
- sautéed vegetables
- roasted red peppers
- ... in fact almost anything sweet or savoury!

Now get crêping

5 Get a medium-sized pan nice and hot over high heat. Lightly grease with butter, then add enough of the batter to **thinly** cover the pan (crêpes must be thin). Tilt the pan to get an even spread, **cook for about a minute.** Flip it over for another minute and voila! Now repeat until you have a nice stack of crêpes ready to work with.

6 When you're ready to serve, place a crêpe into your warm, buttered pan and add your filling on one side. **Fold the crêpe in half** (over the filling), then into a quarter, if you like. Warm it gently and it's ready to eat. Get 'em while they're hot!

c'est magnifique!

Create a signature dish

Stamp your own identity on the ubiquitous crêpe — **invent something** that will have people lining up for more. Here are some ideas just for you … (we won't tell anyone else!)

- Popping candy and lemon juice
- White chocolate and raspberry jam
- Pistachios and vanilla yogurt

Flaming crepes!

You need **fuel and flame** for this. For fuel, use rum, Cointreau or brandy. Heat a metal ladle over the flame, then move it away and pour some of your chosen spirit into it. Take it back over the flame and warm it a little. **Then set it alight with a match!** Carry the flaming ladle to where you're serving the crêpes and gently pour the fiery liquid over them.

Starting a business? What's it called?

Resist the obvious (Crêpe Expectations) and look for that little bit of je ne sais quoi …

- **Crêpe You Out!**
- **Batter Up!**
- **Parlez-vous Crêpe?**
- Actually, **Crêpe Expectations** isn't that bad after all.

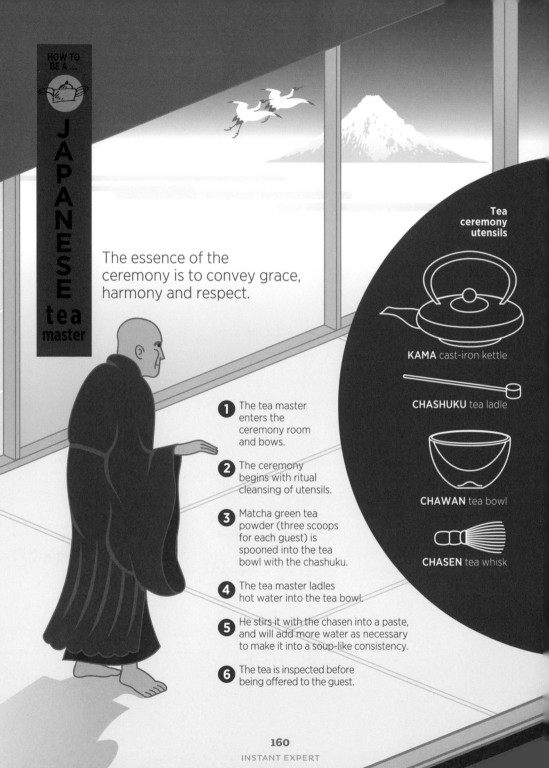

JAPANESE tea master

The essence of the ceremony is to convey grace, harmony and respect.

1 The tea master enters the ceremony room and bows.

2 The ceremony begins with ritual cleansing of utensils.

3 Matcha green tea powder (three scoops for each guest) is spooned into the tea bowl with the chashuku.

4 The tea master ladles hot water into the tea bowl.

5 He stirs it with the chasen into a paste, and will add more water as necessary to make it into a soup-like consistency.

6 The tea is inspected before being offered to the guest.

Tea ceremony utensils

KAMA cast-iron kettle

CHASHUKU tea ladle

CHAWAN tea bowl

CHASEN tea whisk

和

Essential to
tea ceremonies are
hanging scrolls,
which display words
such as *Respect,
Purity, Tranquility,*
and, as here,
← *Harmony.*

7 The guest takes the tea, bows and
returns to a position on the floor.

8 The tea is swallowed in one go.

9 Etiquette dictates that the
guest should admire
the bowl and ask about
its provenance.

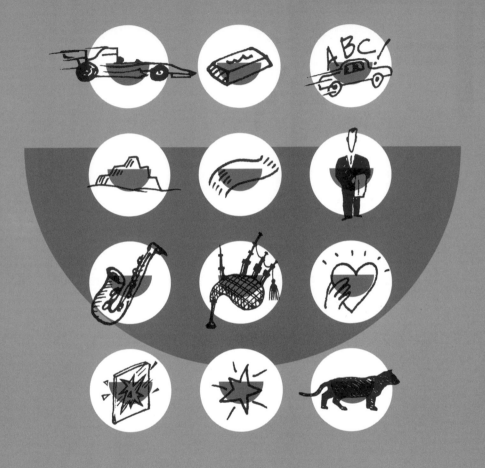

FUN STUFF

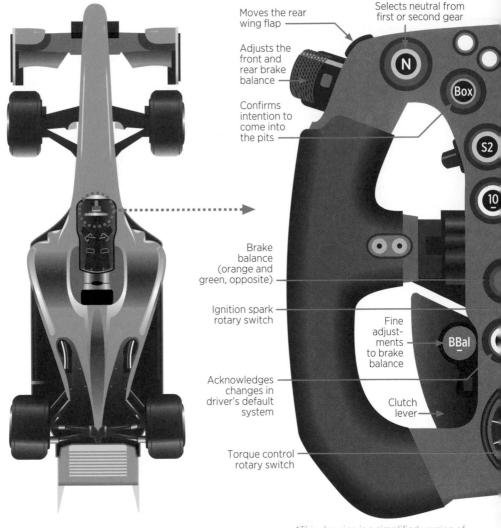

HOW
TO BE
A ...

Formula One driver

In an F1 car you lie down to drive. Wait, that's the steering wheel?
Probably a good idea to get familiar with it right away!

Bird's eye view of an F1 car ... and how you control it*

Moves the rear
wing flap

Selects neutral from
first or second gear

Adjusts the
front and
rear brake
balance

Confirms
intention to
come into
the pits

Brake
balance
(orange and
green, opposite)

Ignition spark
rotary switch

Fine
adjust-
ments
to brake
balance

Acknowledges
changes in
driver's default
system

Clutch
lever

Torque control
rotary switch

*This drawing is a simplified version of
the steering wheel in Sauber F1 team cars.

N

Box

S2

10

BBal

164

INSTANT EXPERT

Activates the driver's radio transmission

S1 and S2 (opposite) can be programmed for various functions

Activates the speed limit for pit entry

Controls energy storage system: either generating or consuming energy

System messages

7
Gear

295
KPM

Shift (this side: +1, opposite: -1)

7

This LED indicates the driver channel is transmitting

Controls rate of fuel consumption

Clutch lever

Oil

BP

Transfers oil from auxiliary to main tank

Multi-function rotary switch allows driver to operate systems without dedicated buttons

Tyre rotary switch

Next: Overtaking →

How to overtake

① Slipstreaming

The red car acts as a battering ram, punching through the air in front of it. This reduces the air pressure in front of the blue car, allowing its engine to work less while keeping the same speed.

Blue follows close behind red, waiting for the opportunity to duck out and overtake on the inside.

What the signalling flags mean

When a signal is intended for one particular car, a sign with the car's number accompanies the flag.

Dangerous situation on the track— **no overtaking**

Slippery track— **slow down**

Slow vehicle on track (such as an ambulance)— **slow down**

Race stopped because of extreme danger

When waved: you are **about to be lapped— must let car pass**

❷ Out-braking

Approaching a corner, blue waits longer to brake than red, forcing red to take a wider, slower line.

But there's no room for blue to miscalculate: if it goes through the turn too quickly, it could end up on the outside of the track, allowing red to cross back to the inside—retaking the lead.

BRAKING HERE

BRAKING HERE

Unsporting behaviour warning (disqualification may follow)

Return to pit (usually because of disqualification)

Return to pit (the team's telemetry has sensed a problem)

Circuit is free from danger

End of race

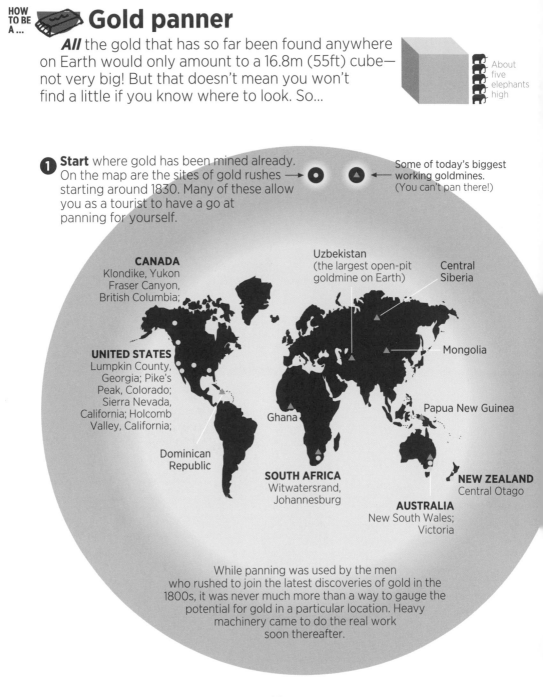

Gold panner

All the gold that has so far been found anywhere on Earth would only amount to a 16.8m (55ft) cube—not very big! But that doesn't mean you won't find a little if you know where to look. So...

About five elephants high

1 **Start** where gold has been mined already. On the map are the sites of gold rushes → starting around 1830. Many of these allow you as a tourist to have a go at panning for yourself.

Some of today's biggest ← working goldmines. (You can't pan there!)

CANADA
Klondike, Yukon
Fraser Canyon,
British Columbia;

Uzbekistan
(the largest open-pit goldmine on Earth)

Central Siberia

UNITED STATES
Lumpkin County,
Georgia; Pike's
Peak, Colorado;
Sierra Nevada,
California; Holcomb
Valley, California;

Mongolia

Papua New Guinea

Ghana

Dominican Republic

SOUTH AFRICA
Witwatersrand,
Johannesburg

NEW ZEALAND
Central Otago

AUSTRALIA
New South Wales;
Victoria

While panning was used by the men who rushed to join the latest discoveries of gold in the 1800s, it was never much more than a way to gauge the potential for gold in a particular location. Heavy machinery came to do the real work soon thereafter.

2 **The panning process** begins with the collection of mud and water from the bottom of a stream where panners have had success before.

3 **Shake the pan** allowing the mud to flow out. Gold is heavier than mud so any gold pieces will sink to the bottom and not be washed out of the pan.

4 You can also work with **the pan slightly submerged in the stream**. As you gently shake the pan any gold will still not be washed away.

5 **Continue** until there's only black sand (and gold!) in your pan. Black sand is magnetic, so if your pan is plastic (best for a beginner), **use a magnet** to lift the sand out, leaving the non-magnetic gold particles.

On-the-road entertainer

HOW TO BE AN ...

The person who can keep everyone happy (especially young children) on a long road trip, is a kind of wizard.

Try these simple games with your tribe.

Banana

Very simple: a point for every yellow vehicle you see. Two points if it's a bulldozer or a bus.

Grocery ABC

The first person says "apple"; the next one repeats "apple" and adds "banana"; the next repeats "apple" and "banana" and adds "cereal" and so on through the alphabet, remembering all the previous items on the list. (Start with avocado if you like— any "A" word.)

Counting cows

Each side of the car counts cows on their side. If there's a cemetery, that side of the car loses all its cows, but only if the other side sees the cemetery and says, "your cows are buried!"

I spy

The classic. You say, "I spy with my little eye, something beginning with T." The rest must guess what it is. Just don't choose stuff that whizzes past too fast.

Always a crowd pleaser: what's the longest placename in the world? (It's a town in Wales.)

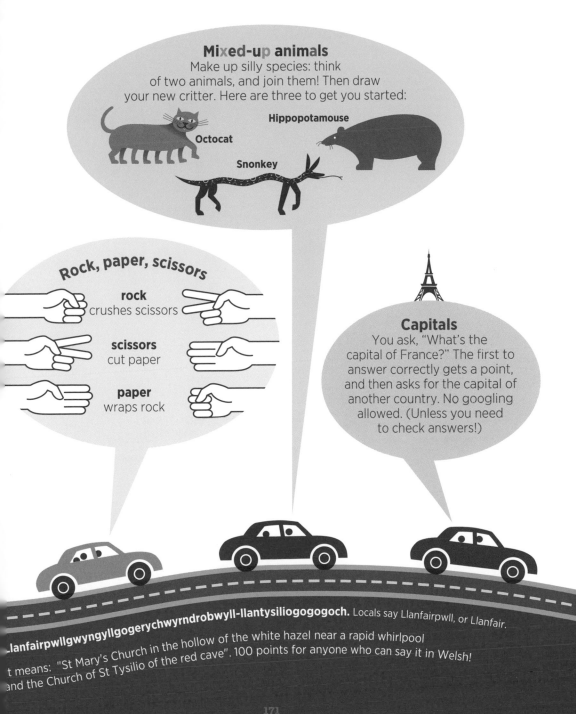

Sand sculptor

Your first effort will probably collapse. Try again.
Practice makes pretty good sand castles.

Getting ready

① The right stuff

The best sand for sculpting is fine. Pick up some wet sand,
squeeze it into a golf ball-sized blob and roll it around in your
hand. If it stays in one piece, it'll be good for building.

② What time is high tide?

And how far does it reach up the beach? Get the local
tide tables. It's a pity when your work is washed away.

③ Essential equipment

Shovel
full-length handle,
small scoop

Compacting buckets ↗
see

Sculpting tools
kitchen spatulas, etc

Heavy piece of wood
for compacting

Water spray bottle
keeps sand damp

Water buckets

④ Bring a picture

Inspiration—something to
work from. Not all castles
look alike. Besides, who said
you have to build a castle?
How about a car? Or an animal?
A giant hot dog? (Why not?)

Compaction is the key

5 Make building blocks

Remove the handle and lid from your compacting bucket.
The best type to use is a plastic 19L (5 gall) with straight sides.

Flip it over and cut a hole in the bottom.

On the beach, shovel in about 10cm (4in) wet sand; add water.

Pack the sand down hard with the wood block. Repeat with sand and water until the cylinder is full.

Tap sides of bucket and lift up.

A perfect compacted building block!

Sculpting

6 Work from the top down

That way the scraped away sand will not
fall on work you've already done.

7 Keep edges crisp

Carve in towards the centre of a shape from
both sides (if you drag a sculpting tool through
a shape, the outside edge tends to fall away).

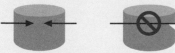

8 Making windows

Outline the shape first, then cut into the
center to get rid of sand, and only then go
in to make the edges neat and sharp.

Carpet dealer

Magic? No, but really beautiful. Experts consider the very best oriental rugs to be Persian. The world's oldest-known example is the Persian Pazyryk carpet, which was discovered in 1949. Carbon dating indicates that it was woven in the 5th century BC.

Where to?

How can you tell what makes an old rug so special?

(And that it is **indeed** old.)

To check authenticity ...

1 **Turn it over.** If it's machine made, there'll be netting on the back.

2 With a magnifying glass, **check the density of the weave;** there should be about 100 stitches for every square centimetre (0.4sq in)

1 sq cm (0.4 sq in)

3 Ask to **burn** an unpicked knot or snippet of fringe; silk and wool smoulder, their substitutes catch alight.

4 **Examine the colour.** The best oriental rugs use natural dyes from vegetables and other sources. You can spot artificial dyes by looking for colours that are markedly stronger than others. Anything orange or pink indicates a manmade rug.

And inspect the weave. The colour in artificial dyes is consistent all the way from the base of the thread to the tip. Natural dyes are more patchy.

Design: abstract symbols or pictures of real things?

Often, motifs are derived from **plants** found in the area where the carpet was made. One of the most common is a twisted teardrop known as the 'boteh'. It's of Persian origin, but the English-speaking world knows it by another name, after it was brought back by colonists: **paisley.**

Modern Afghan war rugs incorporate distinctly untraditional motifs: helicopters and guns.

Know the market

Iran produces about 13 million sq km (5 million sq miles) of carpets annually, and exports them to more than 100 countries. (Hand-woven rugs are one of its main non-oil export items.)

Savvy buyers **avoid the big carpet manufacturing towns** on this map, and head to hidden corners of Iran, Turkey and Syria to find the best deals.

The **most expensive carpet** in the world is a 17th-century Persian rug that was auctioned in London for £21.8m ($33.8m) in 2013.

Butler

At the end of the 1930s, there were 30,000 butlers in Britain. By the 1980s there were perhaps 100. But today, there are estimated to be 5,000 in Britain and two million worldwide, with the greatest demand coming from Asia and the Middle East.

Butler is related to the French *bouteille* (bottle), since the job originally was to look after the cellar. This often represented a sizable amount of the household's assets.

Today, only in the grandest houses do butlers play the role seen in *Upstairs, Downstairs* or *Downton Abbey*. A modern butler is more like a personal valet, more like *Jeeves*, perhaps, rather than being the head of a household with many servants.

Some employers may require this traditional suit (especially for a formal dinner party), but many just want you to dress neatly. It also depends on the climate.

Patience

Patience is not only a virtue, it's essential in butlering. Along with silence, loyalty, car mechanics and good laundry skills, Sir.

Discretion

A good butler ("a man's man") is often a substitute for a wife, but if *your* man has a wife already you may have to negotiate the tricky path between **wife** and other **lady friends.** You'll have to practise your poker face.

Cocktails

Bond wanted his shaken not stirred. (He was right, and the harder the shake the better to get those tiny ice crystals into the drink.) You must know what *your* guy (that is, your master) likes—and all his guests, as well.

Are there butler schools?

Traditionally a man (butlers are typically but not always male) will start in a lower position in the household staff, but there are a number of institutes where you can learn the specifics of the big job.

What's the salary?

Top graduates from the best butlering institutes might start in the £40,000–50,000 range. It does depend on the extent of the job: managers of large estates (and perhaps multiple homes and a yacht) on top of daily butlering can command £150,000 or more.

The best place to find a job?

As the number of millionaires (and billionaires) increases globally, the demand for people to run a family's multiple households has also increased. This is particularly true in the Middle East, China, and India. But the main opportunities are in Britain and the US.

Must I know how to fold napkins?

Don't worry, go to butlersguild.com to find out all about how to make a napkin into a peace lily, a rosebud, a cardinal's hat and many more shapes. I like the simple pyramid, here. →

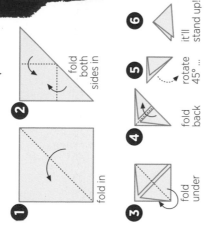

1 fold in

2 fold both sides in

3 fold under

4 fold back

5 rotate 45° ...

6 it'll stand up!

Could I become a *Royal* butler?

On the official website of the The British Monarchy you can find out how to apply for a job in one of the Royal households. Be prepared for extensive background checks. If you are looking for a good salary, working for the Queen won't be your best bet (current salaries for butlers are in the £24,000 range), but you do get somewhere to live, and good health and holiday benefits.

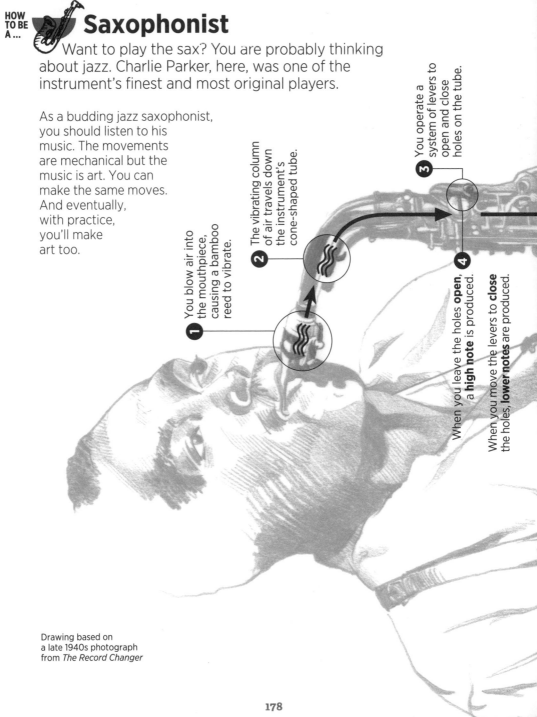

Saxophonist

Want to play the sax? You are probably thinking about jazz. Charlie Parker, here, was one of the instrument's finest and most original players.

As a budding jazz saxophonist, you should listen to his music. The movements are mechanical but the music is art. You can make the same moves. And eventually, with practice, you'll make art too.

1 You blow air into the mouthpiece, causing a bamboo reed to vibrate.

2 The vibrating column of air travels down the instrument's cone-shaped tube.

3 You operate a system of levers to open and close holes on the tube.

4 When you leave the holes **open**, a **high note** is produced.

When you move the levers to **close** the holes, **lower notes** are produced.

Drawing based on a late 1940s photograph from *The Record Changer*

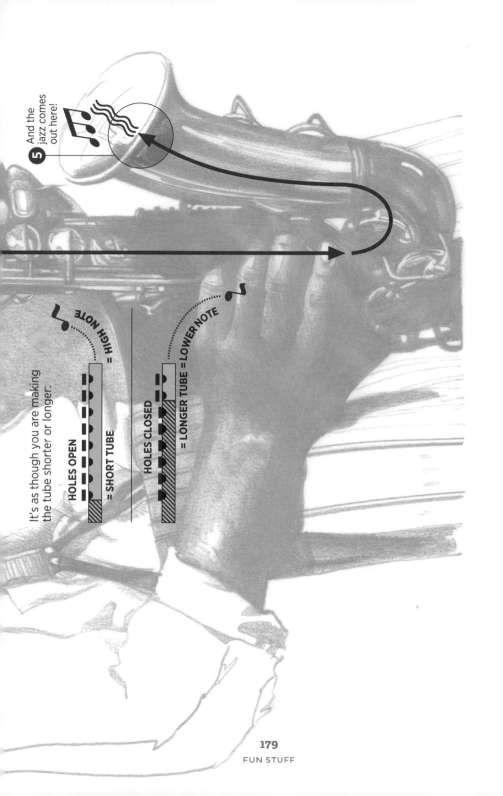

5 And the jazz comes out here!

It's as though you are making the tube shorter or longer:

HOLES OPEN = **SHORT TUBE** = **HIGH NOTE**

HOLES CLOSED = **LONGER TUBE** = **LOWER NOTE**

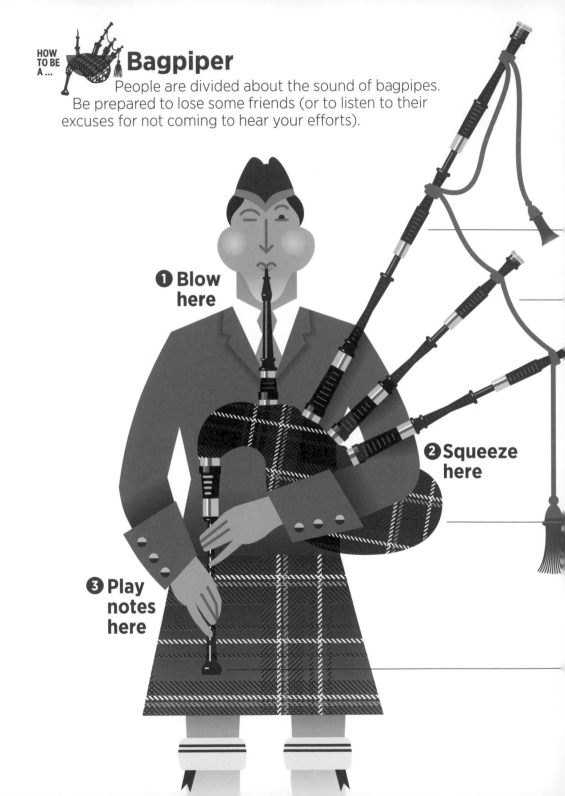

HOW TO BE A ... **Bagpiper**

People are divided about the sound of bagpipes. Be prepared to lose some friends (or to listen to their excuses for not coming to hear your efforts).

❶ Blow here

❷ Squeeze here

❸ Play notes here

It's a difficult instrument.
These steps will help.

- Find an **instructor.**
- Before buying a whole set of pipes, just get a **chanter** (see below).
- **Listen** to different types of pipe music.
- **Practise!** Be patient. Practise again.

The main parts

DRONES

bass

inside tenor

outside tenor

Drone pipes produce the characteristic sound of the pipes — a harmonizing note that continues while the melody is played on the chanter.

Drones consist of two or more sections with sliding joints, so you can adjust the pitch.

The bass drone is usually pitched two octaves below the chanter.

BAG

The engine that drives the music. By blowing air into the bag, and squeezing your elbow against it, you force air through the chanter and drone pipes.

The bag is traditionally made from animal skin, and some still are, but synthetic materials are used more often now. This one is covered in tartan cloth.

CHANTER

The melody pipe. Best to get one with countersunk finger holes.

As well as Scotland, many other cultures developed their own form of bagpipes.

Bulgaria — *kaba gaida*
France — *bagad*
Galicia — *gaita*
Germany — *huemmelchen*
Greece — *tsampouna*
Hungary — *duda*
Southern India — *sruti upanga*
Southern Italy — *zampogna*
Romania — *cimpoi*
Sweden — *säckpipa*
Turkey — *tulum*

Pakistan is the largest manufacturer of bagpipes. In 2010, it was a $6.8 billion industry.

Casanova

Giacomo Casanova was a writer, spy, violinist, Roman Catholic cardinal, magician, alchemist, gambler, prisoner, librarian ... and, oh yes, a womaniser.

If that last bit is what you are interested in, read on: **study the man's technique!** But please beware of cold looks, if not outright hostility, from female friends.

The moves he made

1 Casanova was able to **use his charm** to find women who seemed to be troubled by a jealous boyfriend, or who had other emotional difficulties.*

2 As he befriended a women, he'd give her **advice** about her amorous problems.

3 He charged handsomely for this advice.

4 Pretty soon, he **seduced** the woman.

5 But he always had a plan of escape if the jealous boyfriend returned.

*One successful method for meeting women was to put newspaper advertisements for the "right" person to rent his flat. Casanova did this while living in London in 1763. From the respondents he chose one woman— "Mistress Pauline". He then visited her house to interview her about renting his flat.

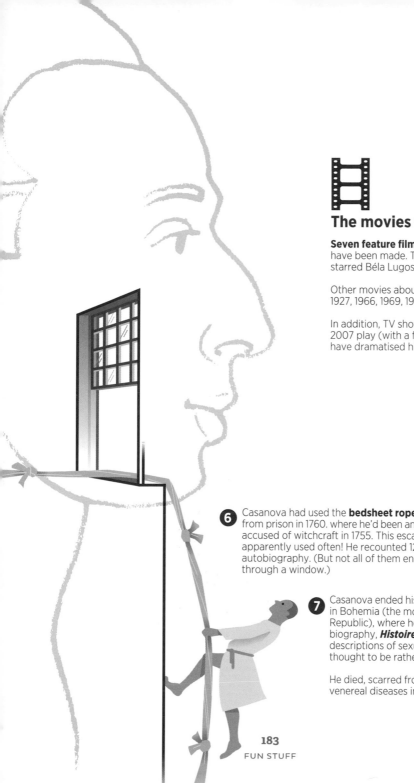

The movies they made

Seven feature films about Casanova have been made. The first, from 1918, starred Béla Lugosi.

Other movies about him appeared in 1927, 1966, 1969, 1976, 1982 and 2005.

In addition, TV shows, an opera and a 2007 play (with a female Casanova) have dramatised his life.

6 Casanova had used the **bedsheet rope trick** to escape from prison in 1760. where he'd been an inmate since being accused of witchcraft in 1755. This escape technique was apparently used often! He recounted 120 affairs in his autobiography. (But not all of them ended with his exit through a window.)

7 Casanova ended his days as a librarian in Bohemia (the modern-day Czech Republic), where he wrote the auto-biography, *Histoire de Ma Vie.* His descriptions of sexual escapades is thought to be rather exaggerated.

He died, scarred from smallpox and venereal diseases in 1798, aged 73.

HOW TO BE A ... Glassmaker

Broken any windows lately? Here's the job for you.
You need sand, plus some rather expensive machinery.

1 There are **four main ingredients** in glassmaking:

Silica
crushed
white
sand

**Sodium
carbonate**
to lower
the melting
point of
sand

**Crushed
limestone**
to stabilise
the mixture

Additives
for colour,
clarity,
weight,
brilliance

2 The ingredients are mixed together in a hopper.

3 The mixture is melted in a furnace.

4 In the float-glass process, molten glass is floated onto a bed of molten tin. The glass spreads out to form a uniform, flat sheet.

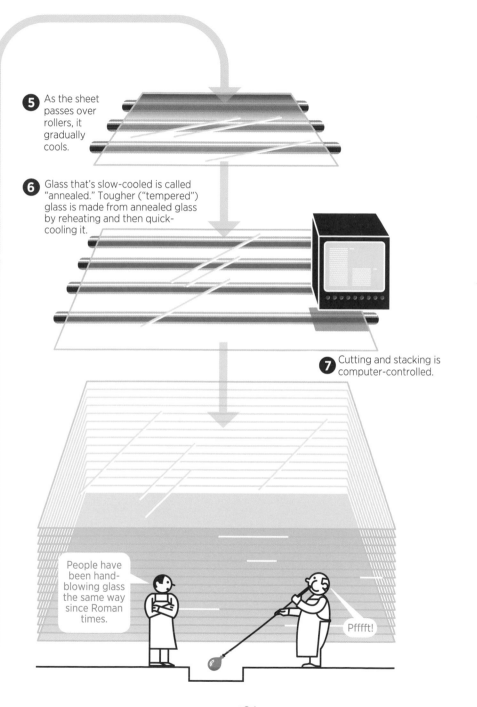

5 As the sheet passes over rollers, it gradually cools.

6 Glass that's slow-cooled is called "annealed." Tougher ("tempered") glass is made from annealed glass by reheating and then quick-cooling it.

7 Cutting and stacking is computer-controlled.

People have been hand-blowing glass the same way since Roman times.

Pfffft!

HOW TO BE AN ...

Astronomer

It's been a long day on the trail. Back at the campsite, lie down and gaze at the night sky.
Are we alone, or is there anyone else out there?

Thinking about extraterrestrial life ...   and looking at ..

In 2014, astronomers at the University of California, Berkeley SETI* Research Center made a presentation to the US Congress about the possibility of other life in space.

Perhaps it's time to say goodbye to Earth, and extend our travel plans a bit!

THE SETI PRESENTATION INCLUDED:

★2,000 exoplanets have been discovered in the last 20 years, thanks to the Kepler space telescopes.

★70% of all stars are accompanied by planets, so there could be one trillion planets in the Milky Way. (And the Milky Way is only one of the 150 billion galaxies visible to our telescopes.)

MILKY WAY

★If just one star in five has a habitable planet orbiting it, the Milky way could be home to anywhere from 10 billion to 80 billion Earth-Ike planets

★**The possibility of extraterrestrial lfe is "close to 100 percent".**

★"The chance of finding [life] ... will happen in the next 20 years depending on the financing".

*Search for Extraterrestrial Intelligence

INSTANT EXPERT

shooting stars
Actually, they aren't stars at all!
(They are stray bits of space debris from a comet's tail.)

DISTANCE
Most meteors become visible about 80km (50 miles) up, and vaporise totally by 8km (5 miles) above Earth.

SPEED
Outside Earth's atmosphere, meteors travel at 210,000km/h (130,000mph).

FRICTION
When space debris—even an object **the size of a pea**—slams into Earth's atmosphere at this speed, the resulting friction generates heat that vaporises the debris and causes the flash of light that is the tail of a "shooting star."

"Meteor"
refers to the tail.

"Meteoroid" is the space debris that is vaporised.

"Meteorite" is the name for a meteoroid that does not burn up but falls all the way to Earth.

Dad, how can you see **a pea** that far up in the sky?

What you see is the **tail.** It's only about 1m (3ft) wide, but it's a few kilometres long.

actual size of a typical meteoroid

Cat

Late-night cat parties, bringing dead mice indoors, casual indifference... oh, yes, those are all important ingredients of feline life, but as a cat, we must never forget our credo: **total independence!**

Here's how to behave:

1 Treat humans with as much **disdain** as possible.

2 If we do need attention, brush up to the owner's leg. He or she will think it's cute. But what we're doing is reversing that "owner" thing. We'll be leaving **pheromones** on the leg, and that's **our mark of ownership.** Other animals will keep away when they sense we've been there first.

We've got **pheromones** in our cheeks, chin, mouth, forehead, paws and near the back end.

3 If we bring dead animals into the house, remember that humans will think we are a clever hunter, not that it's a big hint that we are **hungry.** (What, eat the dead thing? Yuck! Never!)

4 **Hiss** a lot. Does not apply to feline friends (BFFs).

5 **Scare birds** by staring at them from nearby bushes. We may never get one, but just being threatening is fun, isn't it?

6 **Empty boxes** are great play houses. We feel a sense of security in them. Just never get into a box labelled *Shrödinger.**

*We might die, or not die; it's a bit too complicated to explain this in a footnote. Look up *Shrödinger's Cat.*

7 The **tail** is our mood index. Up = happy; limp = so-so; down = get me a valium.

How humans say *meow* in different languages

Funny how they try to mimic us, isn't it?

miau Belarusian, Croatian, Hungarian, Dutch, Finnish, Lithuanian, Malay, German, Polish, Russian, Portuguese, Romanian, Spanish

mnau Czech

meong Indonesian

niau Ukranian

niaou Greek

miaou French

nya Japanese

miav/miao Danish, Norwegian, Swedish

mjá Icelandic

ya-ong Korean

miya'un Urdu

meo-meo Vietnamese

mao Chinese (it's also the Chinese word for cat)

This is what we might look like after rolling in, and chewing catnip. There's a chemical compound in it that gives us cats a nice, brief high.

INDEX

INDEX

INDEX

INDEX

INDEX

Sources

The web

wikipedia.org; wikihow.com; thehoneybeeconservancy.org; organicauthority.com; savebees.org; tapmytrees.com; cen.ulaval.ca; rugs-oriental.net; kodak.com; healthcommunities.com; dogwalker.com; highered.mcgraw-hill.com; npr.org; studio360.org; theguardian.com; makemysushi.com;hikelight.com; horsejobs.ca; nasa.gov; climate.gov; epa.gov; good.is; fullthrottlenyne.org; ridemyown.com; howstuffworks.com; baristahq.com; oceanservice.noaa.gov; worldatlas.com; water.usgs.gov; fitnessmagazine.com; talklikeapirate.com; ehow.com; goldgold.com; geology.com; mining.com; gold-traders.co.uk; carpetencyclopedia.com; japanese-tea-ceremony.net; time.com; massagetherapytrends.com; firstpeoplesofcanada.com; butlersguild.com; royal.gov.uk; origamiway.com; enologyinternational.com; webmd.com; genuinemaoricuisine.com; gacc.nifc.gov; earthobservatory.nasa.gov; piping.on.ca; ecometrica.com; scottishheavyathletics.com; odditycentral.com; theweatherprediction.com; wired.com; billzart.wordpress.com;

Books, magazines and oganizations

The Sibley Guide to Birds, David Sibley; Birds of the World, Colin Harrison and Alan Greensmith; *National Geographic Atlas of the World; Mr. Boston Deluxe Official Bartender's Guide; Bitters,* Brad Thomas Parsons; *How to Cook Everything,* Mark Bittman; *Diagnostic Tests for Men; The American Medical Association Encyclopedia of Medicine; Life on Man,* Theodor Rosebury; *A Pictorial History of Jazz,* Orrin Keepknews and Bill Grauer, Jr.; *The Sivananda Companion to Yoga; The Dog Owner's Manual,* Dr. David Brunner and Sam Stall; *Mammals,* Juliet Clutton-Brock; *Total Immersion,* Terry Laughlin; *Time; Attaché; Sports Illustrated; The Smallest-Ever Guide to Cocktails; Backpacker;* Escape Sailboats; Shelburne Farms

Acknowledgements

There's just one name on the cover of this book, but if all the names of all the people who have contributed to the making of it were included, there'd be no room for art. And we need art, right?

So here's who should be listed along with the "author." Please forgive me if I have forgotten to include anyone.

Ben Handicott in Australia and Piers Pickard in London—both of whom I worked with on a "sister" book to this one, called *The Book Of Everything*—first floated the idea of *Instant Expert*. Thank you for asking me to do another book with Lonely Planet.

Robin Barton—the project manager on *The Book Of Everything*—moved from Australia to England where he fielded my nagging questions about content for *Instant Expert* and my fear that not being an expert in anything at all would be all too apparent. What on earth made me think I could do a book that purported to help readers become experts? Well, it was a struggle but somehow the thing was completed. I understand a bit better what it must be like to be a commissioning editor at a very busy publisher. Thank you, Robin.

Robin also proofread the book, reminding me about proper English spelling and grammar that I'm afraid I lost somewhere in the middle of the Atlantic.

Ben Handicott stepped up to be a long-distance colleague again, to help with research when it looked as though I'd miss the deadline. Thanks Ben!

Thank you to Don George for the *How to be a Travel Writer* piece—I'm certainly no expert on that. Thank you to Matthias Alfen for terrific artistic advice and conversations about ideas that I didn't think would work, and to Geraldine Marcenyac for correcting my French.

Ooo, la la!

Apologies to friends and family whose invitations to dinner, or more, were refused for months on end. Grumpiness is not a nice trait, but it seems to rear up during the countdown to the final delivery of words and pictures.

Afraid not... *sorry* *not yet* *NO!*

Over the years, I have been lucky to have been commissioned by great art directors, and parts of some of the graphics in the book have appeared in different forms in their magazines. Thank you to Paul Carstensen, Ann Harvey, Miranda Dempster, Rudy Hoglund, Steve Hoffman, Holly Holliday, Owen Phillips and Robert Priest.

Last word for my dear Erin. As ever, you looked at everything carefully and weren't shy about telling me what needed clarification. And as ever, you were always right, dammit! Thank *you.*

2014

About the author

Born in England, Nigel Holmes studied illustration at the Royal College of Art in London and then freelanced for magazines and newspapers for 12 years before going to America in 1978 to work for *Time* magazine.

He became graphics director and stayed there for 16 years. Since 1994 he has run his own business, Explanation Graphics, explaining all sorts of things for a variety of clients. These have included American Express, the Bertelsmann Foundation, the Smithsonian Institution, Taschen and United Heathcare.

He also creates information graphics and illustrations for publications such as the *Atlantic, National Geographic* and the *New York Times.*

He has written seven books on aspects of information design, and a children's book *Pinhole and the Expedition to the Jungle.*

His first book for Lonely Planet, *The Book of Everything,* won a silver medal from the Society of American Travel Writers. Other prizes include the Lifetime Achievement Award from the Society of News Design.

With his son, Rowland, he makes short animated films for clients that have included the TED Conference, *Fortune* magazine's Brainstorm Conference, Good Magazine and the National Geographic Society.

He always wears **blue.**

Goodbye!
Thank you for looking!

IMPRINT

LONELY PLANET'S
INSTANT EXPERT

Publishing Director Piers Pickard
Project Manager Robin Barton
Cover Mark Adams
Layout Designer Laura Jane
Print Production Larissa Frost
Thanks to Brendan Dempsey, Ben Handicott, Karyn Noble

November 2014
ISBN 978 1 74321 999 7

Published by
Lonely Planet Publications Pty Ltd
ABN 36 005 607 983
90 Maribyrnong St, Footscray,
Victoria, 3011, Australia
www.lonelyplanet.com

Printed in China
1 0 9 8 7 6 5 4 3 2
© Lonely Planet 2014

Lonely Planet Offices
Australia Locked Bag 1,
Footscray, Victoria, 3011
Phone - 03 8379 8000
Email - talk2us@lonelyplanet.com.au

USA 150 Linden St, Oakland, CA 94607
Phone - 510 250 6400
Toll free - 800 275 8555
Email - info@lonelyplanet.com

United Kingdom Media Centre,
201 Wood Lane, London W12 7TQ
Phone - 020 8433 1333
Email - go@lonelyplanet.co.uk

Although the authors and Lonely Planet have taken all reasonable care in preparing this book, we make no warranty about the accuracy or completeness of its content and, to the maximum extent permitted, disclaim all liability arising from its use. All outdoor activities (as well as some of the other activities in this book) carry an inherent degree of risk. None of the information in this book is intended to provide comprehensive guidance or advice and we recommend that anyone participating in these activities be aware of the risks involved and seek professional instruction and guidance. Also, none of the health/medical information in this book is intended as a substitute for professional medical advice; always seek the advice of a qualified practitioner.

Paper in this book is certified against the Forest Stewardship Council™ standards. FSC™ promotes environmentally responsible, socially beneficial and economically viable management of the world's forests.